# Sufi Secrets Of Inner Healing

## Embracing Emotional and Spiritual Well-being in Islam

By:

## Hanifa Ibn Al-Nawawi

# Copyright © 2023 by Hanifa Ibn Al-Nawawi

All rights reserved. No part of this publication may be reproduced, distributed, or transmitted in any form or by any means, including photocopying, recording, or other electronic or mechanical methods, without the prior written permission of the publisher, except in the case of brief quotations embodied in critical reviews and certain other noncommercial uses permitted by copyright law.

*Sufi Secrets to Inner Healing…………*

# TABLE OF CONTENTS

Copyright © 2023 by Hanifa Ibn Al-Nawawi .................2
Dedication ................................................................6
Book Description ......................................................7
Introduction ............................................................10
*Chapter One* ..........................................................18
Section 1.1: Introduction to Sufism: The Path of Love and Healing ...................................................................18
Section 1.2 Understanding the Essence of Sufism ......23
Section 1.3: The Journey of the Sufi Seeker ..............27
Section 1.4: Uniting the Heart and Spirit ..................32
*Chapter Two* ..........................................................37
Section 2.1: The Healing Power of Remembrance (Dhikr).......37
Section 2.2: Dhikr: A Pathway to Spiritual Connection............44
Section 2.3: The Benefits of Dhikr in Healing the Soul. ..........50
Section 2.3: Practices of Dhikr for Emotional and Spiritual Well-being..................................................56
*Chapter Three* ......................................................62
Section 3.1: Purifying the Heart: The Key to Inner Healing. ....62

*Sufi Secrets to Inner Healing*…………

Section 3.2: Recognizing the Diseases of the Heart ................. 68

Section 3.3: Tazkiyah: The Art of Purification ....................... 75

Section 3.4: The Virtues and Remedies for a Pure Heart ......... 82

*Chapter Four* ............................................................................. 88

Section 4.1: Unveiling the Beloved: Love as the Ultimate Healer. ..................................................................................... 88

Section 4.3: The Role of Love in Spiritual Transformation .... 102

Section 4.3: The Manifestations of Love in Sufi Poetry and Literature ............................................................................. 109

*Chapter Five* ............................................................................ 113

Section 5.1: The Inner Journey of Self-Reflection and Self-Knowledge. ......................................................................... 113

Section 5.2: the Self-Exploration in the Light of Islamic Teachings ............................................................................ 117

Section 5.3: The Significance of Self-Awareness on the Spiritual Path ..................................................................................... 124

Section 5.4: the Practices for Deepening Self-Knowledge and Finding Inner Healing ......................................................... 132

*Chapter Six* .............................................................................. 139

Section 6.1: Surrendering to Divine Will: Finding Peace in Acceptance .......................................................................... 139

*Sufi Secrets to Inner Healing*...........

Section 6.2: The Understanding the Concept of Divine Will (Qadr) .................................................................. 143
Section 6.3: Embracing Acceptance and Letting Go ............... 147
Section 6.3: Attaining Inner Peace through Surrender ............ 151
*Chapter Seven* ........................................................................ 155
Section 7.1: Arabic Wisdom: Exploring Sacred Texts and Their Healing Messages .................................................................... 155
Section 7.2: The Quranic Verses of Healing and Solace ......... 159
Section 7.3: Hadiths on Emotional and Spiritual Well-being .. 163
Section 7.4: the Beauty and Depth of Arabic Calligraphy ...... 167
*Chapter Eight* ......................................................................... 171
Section 8.1: The Sufi Path to Compassion and Service .......... 171
Section 8.2: Compassion as a Transformative Force .............. 178
Section 8.3: The Relationship between Selflessness and Inner Healing ..................................................................................... 184
Section 8.4: Engaging in Acts of Service and Kindness ......... 191
*Chapter Nine* .......................................................................... 198
Section 9.1: The Dance of Whirling: A Sacred Expression of Healing and Unity ................................................................... 198
Section 9.2: Understanding Sama: The Whirling Meditation . 205

*Sufi Secrets to Inner Healing*………..

Section 9.3: Symbolism and Significance of the Whirling Dance ............................................................................... 209

Section 9.4: Experiencing Wholeness and Unity through Sama ............................................................................... 216

*Chapter Ten* ............................................................................ 220

Section 10.1: Conclusion: Living a Life of Inner Healing and Spiritual Well-being ............................................................ 220

Section 10.2: In the name of Allah, the Most Gracious, the Most Merciful ................................................................................ 227

Section 10.3: Emotional and Spiritual Balance ...................... 234

Section 10.4: The Eternal Journey of Inner Healing and Transformation ....................................................................... 241

Appreciation ............................................................................ 249

*Sufi Secrets to Inner Healing............*

# Dedication

To the seekers of truth, the passionate souls on a quest for inner healing and spiritual enlightenment. May this book serve as a guiding light on your journey, illuminating the path with wisdom and inspiration. With heartfelt gratitude, I dedicate this work to all those who yearn to deepen their connection with Allah and discover the transformative power of Sufism. May your hearts be filled with peace, your spirits uplifted, and your lives enriched by the profound teachings within these pages.

*Sufi Secrets to Inner Healing...........*

## Book Description

Assalamu Alaikum wa rahmatullahi wa barakatuh.

*Sufi Secrets to Inner Healing: Embracing Emotional and Spiritual Well-being in Islam*

Discover the transformative power of Sufism, the mystical dimension of Islam, and embark on a profound journey of inner healing and spiritual growth. In this inspiring and enlightening book, Islamic scholar [Author's Name] invites you to explore the teachings of Sufi masters and uncover the timeless wisdom of the Holy Quran and Hadiths.

Drawing upon his vast knowledge and personal experiences, [Author's Name] delves into the depths of emotional and spiritual well-being, offering practical insights and profound guidance for those seeking inner peace and tranquility in their lives. Through clear explanations, relatable examples, and the illumination of sacred texts, he shows how the path of Sufism can unlock the hidden treasures of the heart and lead to a deeper connection with Allah.

*Sufi Secrets to Inner Healing...........*

With chapters exploring topics such as self-knowledge, surrender to divine will, compassion, acts of service, and the transformative power of whirling meditation (Sama), this book provides a comprehensive roadmap for cultivating emotional resilience, nurturing the soul, and experiencing profound spiritual transformation.

Whether you are a devoted follower of Islam or someone seeking universal wisdom, this book will empower you to embrace the path of emotional and spiritual well-being. It serves as a guiding light, revealing the beauty and depth of Islamic teachings, and showing how they can be applied in everyday life to find solace, healing, and a profound sense of purpose.

Step onto the path of Sufism and embark on a life-changing journey toward inner healing and spiritual enlightenment. Allow Sufi Secrets to Inner Healing to illuminate your path, inspire your soul, and guide you to the abundant blessings and peace that await those who seek them.

*Sufi Secrets to Inner Healing………..*

# Introduction

**Bismillahir Rahmanir Raheem**

*Sufi Secrets to Inner Healing - Embracing Emotional and Spiritual Well-being in Islam*

Assalamu Alaikum wa rahmatullahi wa barakatuh.

Dear brothers and sisters,

I begin by praising Allah, the Most Merciful, and sending peace and blessings upon His beloved Prophet Muhammad (peace be upon him). It is with great joy and humility that I pick my paper and pen to share insights through a book titled:

**"Sufi Secrets to Inner Healing:**

***Embracing Emotional and Spiritual Well-being in Islam."***

In this book, I aim to explore the profound teachings of Sufism, a mystical dimension of Islam that focuses on the purification of the heart and the attainment of spiritual excellence. Sufism offers a transformative path that guides us towards inner healing, emotional well-being, and a deeper connection with Allah.

*Sufi Secrets to Inner Healing………..*

As an Islamic scholar with a deep understanding of the Holy Quran and the traditions of our beloved Prophet (peace be upon him), I have witnessed the immense wisdom and guidance found within these sacred sources. It is through these teachings that we discover the keys to unlocking our spiritual potential and experiencing true inner peace.

The Quran, the ultimate source of divine revelation, contains numerous verses that address the significance of emotional and spiritual well-being. Allah says in Surah Al-Baqarah (Chapter 2), verse 152:

"So remember Me; I will remember you. And be grateful to Me and do not deny Me."

This verse reminds us of the importance of remembrance, gratitude, and acknowledging our Creator. Through connecting with Allah and expressing gratitude for His blessings, we cultivate a state of inner peace and contentment.

Furthermore, the Hadith literature, which consists of the sayings and actions of our beloved Prophet Muhammad (peace be upon

*Sufi Secrets to Inner Healing…………*

him), provides practical guidance on emotional and spiritual well-being. The Prophet (peace be upon him) said:

"Indeed, in the body, there is a piece of flesh which, if it is sound, the whole body is sound, and if it is corrupt, the whole body is corrupt. Indeed, it is the heart."

This Hadith emphasizes the pivotal role of the heart in our overall well-being. By purifying and nurturing our hearts, we can experience transformative healing and establish a strong connection with Allah.

In this book, I draw upon the profound teachings of Sufi masters and scholars who have illuminated the path of inner healing and spiritual well-being. Their wisdom, combined with the timeless guidance of the Quran and the Hadith, serves as a roadmap for us to navigate the challenges of our modern lives and attain true inner peace.

Throughout my journey as an Islamic scholar and seasoned preacher, I have witnessed the transformative power of embracing emotional and spiritual well-being. I have seen

*Sufi Secrets to Inner Healing………..*

individuals find solace and healing by turning to Allah, seeking His forgiveness, and engaging in acts of worship and devotion. The teachings of Sufism have played a significant role in guiding them towards a deeper understanding of themselves and their relationship with Allah.

Dear brothers and sisters, the journey of inner healing and spiritual well-being is one that requires sincerity, effort, and constant self-reflection. It is a journey of self-discovery, self-discipline, and seeking closeness to Allah. Through this book, I hope to inspire and empower you to embark on this transformative path and experience the profound healing that comes from surrendering to the divine.

May Allah, the Most Merciful, guide us all on this journey of inner healing and spiritual well-being. May He grant us the wisdom and strength to embrace our emotions, purify our hearts, and draw closer to Him. May this book serve as a source of inspiration and enlightenment for all who seek to unlock the Sufi secrets to inner healing.

*Sufi Secrets to Inner Healing………..*

Dear brothers and sisters,

As we delve into the chapters of this book, we will explore various aspects of emotional and spiritual well-being through the lens of Sufism. We will uncover the profound teachings that emphasize self-awareness, self-reflection, and self-transformation. We will learn how to embrace our emotions, recognize their messages, and channel them in a way that aligns with our spiritual growth.

The Sufi path teaches us that by cultivating qualities such as love, compassion, patience, and forgiveness, we can attain a state of inner balance and harmony. These virtues are beautifully encapsulated in the words of Allah in Surah Ar-Rum (Chapter 30), verse 21:

"And among His Signs is that He created for you mates from among yourselves, that you may dwell in tranquility with them, and He has put love and mercy between your hearts. Surely in that are signs for those who reflect."

*Sufi Secrets to Inner Healing...........*

This verse reminds us of the importance of cultivating love and mercy in our relationships, not only with our spouses but with all those around us. By nurturing these qualities, we create an environment of tranquility and peace, both within ourselves and in our interactions with others.

Additionally, the teachings of Sufism emphasize the significance of spiritual practices such as dhikr (remembrance of Allah), meditation, and seeking solitude to deepen our connection with the Divine. The Quran states in Surah Al-Jumu'ah (Chapter 62), verse 10:

"And when the prayer is ended, then disperse in the land and seek of Allah's bounty, and remember Allah much, that ye may be successful."

This verse encourages us to engage in acts of remembrance and reflection after our prayers, seeking the abundant blessings of Allah and nourishing our souls. Through these spiritual practices, we can attain a state of tranquility, find solace in the remembrance of Allah, and experience inner healing.

*Sufi Secrets to Inner Healing…………*

As we progress through the chapters, I will share personal anecdotes and reflections from my own journey as an Islamic scholar and seasoned preacher. I have witnessed the transformative power of embracing Sufi teachings in my own life and the lives of others. I have seen individuals find solace, healing, and spiritual growth by incorporating these principles into their daily lives.

Dear brothers and sisters, as we embark on this journey together, let us approach it with open hearts and minds. Let us strive to integrate the teachings of Sufism into our daily lives, embracing emotional and spiritual well-being as an integral part of our faith. May this book serve as a guide, illuminating the path to inner healing, spiritual growth, and a deeper connection with Allah.

In conclusion, I pray that Allah, the Most Merciful, blesses our endeavors to embrace emotional and spiritual well-being in the light of Sufi teachings. May He grant us the wisdom, strength, and sincerity to embark on this transformative journey. May this

*Sufi Secrets to Inner Healing…………*

book inspire us to cultivate a state of inner peace, radiate compassion and love, and become beacons of light in our communities.

Assalamu Alaikum wa rahmatullahi wa barakatuh.

*Sufi Secrets to Inner Healing…………*

# *Chapter One*

## Section 1.1: Introduction to Sufism: The Path of Love and Healing

In the name of Allah, the Most Gracious, the Most Merciful.

Praise be to Allah, the Lord of all worlds, and blessings and peace be upon our beloved Prophet Muhammad (peace be upon him) and his family and companions.

Dear brothers and sisters in Islam, let us embark on a journey to explore the profound teachings of Sufism - the path of love and healing within the folds of Islam. Sufism invites us to delve into the depths of our hearts and souls, seeking a direct and intimate connection with Allah, the Most High.

Understanding the Essence of Sufism: Sufism, also known as tasawwuf, is the spiritual dimension of Islam. It is deeply rooted in the Quranic teachings and the practices of our beloved Prophet Muhammad (peace be upon him). Sufism focuses on the inner dimensions of faith, transcending mere rituals and forms,

*Sufi Secrets to Inner Healing…………*

in order to establish a profound and transformative relationship with Allah.

Allah says in the Quran: "But remember Allah with all your hearts" (Surah Al-A'raf, 7:205). This verse emphasizes the significance of engaging in the remembrance of Allah with utmost sincerity and devotion. Sufism emphasizes the inner journey of the heart, enabling us to develop a profound love for Allah and a deep understanding of His divine attributes.

The Journey of the Sufi Seeker: The path of Sufism is a spiritual journey of seeking closeness to Allah and experiencing His divine presence. It is a path of self-reflection, purification, and self-transformation. The Sufi seeker, also known as the murid, strives to purify their heart from spiritual ailments and egoistic desires, in order to attain spiritual enlightenment and nearness to Allah.

One of the key principles of Sufism is the concept of fanaa and baqaa, which means annihilation in the Divine and subsistence in Him. The Sufi seeker seeks to dissolve their ego and worldly

*Sufi Secrets to Inner Healing………..*

attachments, surrendering themselves completely to the will of Allah, and finding solace and fulfillment in His divine presence.

Uniting the Heart and Spirit: Sufism teaches us the importance of aligning our hearts and spirits with the teachings of Islam. It emphasizes the integration of knowledge, love, and action in our spiritual journey. The Sufi path is not separate from the teachings of the Quran and the Sunnah, but rather a deepening and embodiment of those teachings.

The Prophet Muhammad (peace be upon him) said: "Verily, Allah does not look at your outward appearances and wealth, but He looks at your hearts and your deeds" (Sahih Muslim). This Hadith reminds us that the state of our hearts and the sincerity of our intentions hold greater importance in the sight of Allah than external forms and superficialities.

Sufism encourages acts of devotion such as prayer, fasting, charity, and pilgrimage, but with an emphasis on the inner dimensions of these acts. It calls us to perform these acts with

*Sufi Secrets to Inner Healing………..*

presence of heart, love, and sincerity, to cultivate a deep connection with Allah.

Conclusion: Dear brothers and sisters, Sufism is a path of love and healing within Islam. It is a journey that invites us to connect with Allah on a profound level, purify our hearts, and align our spirits with the teachings of the Quran and the Sunnah. By delving into the depths of our hearts, practicing remembrance of Allah, and seeking spiritual enlightenment, we can experience the transformative power of Sufism in our lives.

May Allah guide us on the path of Sufism, grant us the ability to purify our hearts, and shower us with His divine love and mercy. Ameen.

And Allah knows best. Wa-Salaamu Alaikum warahmatullahi wabarakatuh

*Sufi Secrets to Inner Healing…………*

## Section 1.2 Understanding the Essence of Sufism
Bismillahir Rahmanir Rahim.

Dear brothers and sisters in Islam, let us delve into the profound essence of Sufism - the spiritual path that encapsulates the inner dimensions of faith. Sufism invites us to embark on a journey of love, knowledge, and spiritual transformation, guided by the teachings of the Quran and the practices of our beloved Prophet Muhammad (peace be upon him).

Sufism in the Light of the Quran: Sufism finds its roots in the Quran, the divine book of guidance. It draws inspiration from various Quranic verses that illuminate the path of spiritual enlightenment. Allah says in the Quran: "And remember your Lord within yourself in humility and in fear without being apparent in speech - in the mornings and the evenings. And do not be among the heedless" (Surah Al-A'raf, 7:205). This verse emphasizes the importance of engaging in the remembrance of Allah with utmost sincerity and devotion. Sufism encourages

*Sufi Secrets to Inner Healing...........*

believers to immerse themselves in the remembrance of Allah, seeking His divine presence and guidance.

Additionally, Allah states in the Quran: "Verily, in the remembrance of Allah do hearts find rest" (Surah Ar-Ra'd, 13:28). This verse beautifully encapsulates the essence of Sufism, highlighting the deep tranquility and solace that can be found through the remembrance of Allah. Sufism teaches us to cultivate a profound love for Allah, seeking His nearness and finding solace in His divine presence.

Sufism in the Light of the Sunnah: The practices of Sufism are deeply rooted in the life and teachings of our beloved Prophet Muhammad (peace be upon him). The Prophet (peace be upon him) said: "Whoever knows himself knows his Lord" (Sunan Ibn Majah). This Hadith signifies the importance of self-awareness and introspection, key elements in the Sufi path. Sufism encourages believers to delve deep into their inner selves, recognizing their strengths, weaknesses, and spiritual

*Sufi Secrets to Inner Healing………..*

aspirations, in order to establish a profound connection with Allah.

Furthermore, the Prophet Muhammad (peace be upon him) said: "I was sent to perfect noble character" (Musnad Ahmad). This Hadith highlights the emphasis Sufism places on the development of noble character and moral virtues. Sufis strive to embody the beautiful qualities exemplified by the Prophet Muhammad (peace be upon him), such as compassion, patience, humility, and sincerity, as they journey towards spiritual elevation.

The Path of Love and Union: Sufism is often referred to as the path of love, as it emphasizes the profound love and yearning for Allah. Sufis seek to attain a state of divine love and union with the Beloved, recognizing that love is the driving force behind spiritual growth and transformation.

The famous Sufi poet Rumi beautifully encapsulated the essence of Sufism when he said: "Your task is not to seek for love, but merely to seek and find all the barriers within yourself that you

*Sufi Secrets to Inner Healing………..*

have built against it." This poetic expression highlights the need to remove the barriers of the ego, worldly attachments, and negative traits that hinder our journey towards divine love and union.

Conclusion: Dear brothers and sisters, Sufism is a path that leads us to the heart of Islam, embracing the inner dimensions of faith and spirituality. Through the remembrance of Allah, self-reflection, and cultivation of noble character, we can embark on a journey of love and transformation, seeking divine proximity.

And Allah knows best.

Wa allahu ta'ala a

*Sufi Secrets to Inner Healing…………*

## Section 1.3: The Journey of the Sufi Seeker

Bismillahir Rahmanir Rahim (In the name of Allah, the Most Gracious, the Most Merciful).

Dear brothers and sisters in Islam, let us embark on the profound journey of the Sufi seeker - a path of self-discovery, purification, and spiritual elevation. The journey of the Sufi seeker is marked by devotion, introspection, and a deep yearning for closeness to Allah.

The Importance of Seeking: Allah says in the Quran: "And when My servants ask you concerning Me, indeed I am near. I respond to the invocation of the supplicant when he calls upon Me" (Surah Al-Baqarah, 2:186). This verse emphasizes the closeness of Allah to His creation and the importance of seeking Him. The Sufi seeker understands the need to actively seek a connection with Allah, recognizing that true spiritual growth comes from sincere effort and devotion.

The Sufi seeker understands that the journey towards Allah requires dedication and commitment. The Prophet Muhammad

*Sufi Secrets to Inner Healing............*

(peace be upon him) said: "Take one step towards Allah, and He will take ten steps towards you. Walk towards Him, and He will run towards you" (Sahih Muslim). This Hadith beautifully illustrates the reciprocity of the seeker's efforts and Allah's response. By taking the initiative to embark on the journey, the seeker is met with divine grace and blessings.

The Process of Self-Reflection: The journey of the Sufi seeker involves deep introspection and self-reflection. The Prophet Muhammad (peace be upon him) advised: "Take account of yourselves before you are taken to account" (Tirmidhi). This Hadith urges believers to engage in self-assessment, recognizing their strengths and weaknesses, and striving towards self-improvement.

Allah says in the Quran: "O you who have believed, fear Allah and let every soul look to what it has put forth for tomorrow" (Surah Al-Hashr, 59:18). This verse highlights the importance of self-accountability and reflection on our actions. The Sufi seeker diligently examines their intentions, actions, and character traits,

*Sufi Secrets to Inner Healing………..*

seeking to purify their heart and align their desires with the pleasure of Allah.

The Path of Spiritual Purification: The journey of the Sufi seeker involves the purification of the heart and the cultivation of virtuous qualities. Allah says in the Quran: "Indeed, Allah will not change the condition of a people until they change what is in themselves" (Surah Ar-Ra'd, 13:11). This verse emphasizes the transformative power of self-purification and spiritual growth.

The Prophet Muhammad (peace be upon him) said: "Verily, Allah does not look at your outward appearances and wealth, but He looks at your hearts and your deeds" (Sahih Muslim). This Hadith highlights the importance of nurturing a pure heart and performing righteous deeds. The Sufi seeker strives to purify their heart from diseases such as arrogance, jealousy, and greed, replacing them with qualities of humility, contentment, and generosity.

The Union with the Beloved: The ultimate goal of the Sufi seeker is to attain union with the Beloved, to experience a

*Sufi Secrets to Inner Healing...........*

profound connection with Allah. The Prophet Muhammad (peace be upon him) said: "Whosoever knows his self, knows his Lord" (Sunan Ibn Majah). This Hadith reminds the seeker that true knowledge and nearness to Allah come through self-discovery and self-realization.

Allah says in the Quran: "So remember Me; I am confident that I will remember you. Be grateful to Me and do not deny Me." (Surah Al-Baqarah, 2:152). This verse reminds the Sufi seeker of the importance of constant remembrance of Allah, for in His remembrance lies the path to spiritual union.

The Sufi seeker understands that the journey towards union with the Beloved requires steadfastness and perseverance. The Prophet Muhammad (peace be upon him) said: "The one who travels a path in search of knowledge, Allah will make easy for him the path to Paradise" (Sahih Muslim). This Hadith emphasizes the seeker's commitment to seeking knowledge and spiritual growth, as they traverse the path towards Allah.

Conclusion:

*Sufi Secrets to Inner Healing*..........

Dear brothers and sisters, the journey of the Sufi seeker is a transformative and enlightening one. It is a path of seeking, self-reflection, purification, and ultimately, union with the Beloved. By actively seeking Allah's presence, engaging in self-introspection, purifying the heart, and remembering Allah with sincerity, the Sufi seeker embarks on a profound spiritual journey that leads to closeness with the Divine.

Let us strive to be Sufi seekers, dedicated to purifying our hearts, embodying noble qualities, and seeking the eternal love and union with Allah. May Allah guide us on this blessed path and grant us success in our journey of seeking His divine pleasure. Ameen.

And Allah knows best.

*Sufi Secrets to Inner Healing............*

## Section 1.4: Uniting the Heart and Spirit

Assalamu Alaikum wa Rahmatullahi wa Barakatuhu

Dear brothers and sisters in Islam, let us delve into the profound concept of uniting the heart and spirit, a fundamental aspect of the Sufi path. In this chapter, we will explore the importance of harmonizing our inner dimensions, cultivating a deep connection with Allah, and seeking spiritual unity.

The Heart as the Center of Faith: Allah says in the Quran: "The day when there will not benefit [anyone] wealth or children, but only one who comes to Allah with a sound heart" (Surah Ash-Shu'ara, 26:88-89). This verse emphasizes that on the Day of Judgment, the only thing that will truly matter is the state of our hearts. Sufism teaches us that the heart is the center of our faith, the place where the Divine light resides.

The Prophet Muhammad (peace be upon him) said: "Indeed, in the body there is a piece of flesh, which if it is sound, the entire body is sound, and if it is corrupt, the entire body is corrupt. Indeed, it is the heart" (Sahih Bukhari). This Hadith highlights

*Sufi Secrets to Inner Healing...........*

the significance of a pure and sound heart in attaining spiritual well-being. Sufis understand that a purified heart, free from diseases such as envy, pride, and arrogance, is the key to attaining closeness to Allah.

Cultivating Spiritual Awareness: Sufism emphasizes the importance of developing spiritual awareness and mindfulness of Allah's presence in our lives. Allah says in the Quran: "And We have certainly created man and We know what his soul whispers to him, and We are closer to him than [his] jugular vein" (Surah Qaf, 50:16). This verse reminds us that Allah is intimately aware of our thoughts, feelings, and innermost whispers. Sufis strive to be constantly aware of Allah's presence, seeking His guidance and support in every aspect of their lives.

The Prophet Muhammad (peace be upon him) said: "When you stand up to pray, perform your prayer as if it is your last prayer" (Sahih Al-Bukhari). This Hadith emphasizes the importance of being fully present in our acts of worship, engaging our hearts and spirits in prayer. Sufis understand that true spiritual unity

*Sufi Secrets to Inner Healing...........*

can be achieved by immersing ourselves completely in our connection with Allah, transcending the limitations of the physical world.

Seeking the Remembrance of Allah: Allah says in the Quran: "And mention the name of your Lord in the morning and the evening" (Surah Al-Insan, 76:25). This verse reminds us of the importance of constant remembrance of Allah. Sufism teaches us that the remembrance of Allah is a powerful means of uniting the heart and spirit, for it brings us closer to our Creator and instills a sense of tranquility and purpose in our lives.

The Prophet Muhammad (peace be upon him) said: "The likeness of the one who remembers his Lord and the one who does not remember Him is like that of the living and the dead" (Sahih Al-Bukhari). This Hadith emphasizes the transformative power of remembrance, highlighting that true life and vitality are found in remembering Allah. Sufis engage in various forms of remembrance, such as reciting the Quran, chanting the

*Sufi Secrets to Inner Healing…………*

beautiful names of Allah, and engaging in silent contemplation, to strengthen their connection with the Divine.

Conclusion: Dear brothers and sisters, uniting the heart and spirit is a noble endeavor on the path of Sufism. It requires us to cultivate a pure and sound heart, to be aware of Allah's presence in every moment, and to immerse ourselves in the remembrance of our Creator.

By purifying our hearts from negative traits and diseases, we create a space within ourselves for the light of Allah to shine brightly. This purification involves self-reflection, seeking forgiveness, and striving to embody the beautiful qualities taught to us by the Prophet Muhammad (peace be upon him) and exemplified in the lives of the righteous.

Being mindful of Allah's presence in our lives allows us to navigate the trials and tribulations of this world with grace and patience. It reminds us that we are not alone, that our Creator is intimately aware of our struggles and is always near to guide and support us. This awareness helps us develop a deep sense of

*Sufi Secrets to Inner Healing…………*

trust and reliance on Allah, knowing that He is the ultimate source of comfort and solace.

The remembrance of Allah is a powerful tool in uniting our heart and spirit. It is through the remembrance of His name, the recitation of His words in the Quran, and the contemplation of His attributes that we draw closer to Him. The remembrance of Allah brings peace to our souls, uplifts our spirits, and strengthens our connection with the Divine.

Dear brothers and sisters, let us strive to unite our heart and spirit on this beautiful journey of Sufism. May we purify our hearts, be mindful of Allah's presence, and engage in constant remembrance of our Creator. By doing so, we will experience the profound unity and serenity that comes from being in harmony with Allah and His teachings.

May Allah bless us all on this journey and grant us the strength and guidance to unite our heart and spirit. Ameen.

And Allah knows best.

*Sufi Secrets to Inner Healing…………*

# Chapter Two

## Section 2.1: The Healing Power of Remembrance (Dhikr)

بِسْمِ اللَّهِ الرَّحْمَٰنِ الرَّحِيمِ (In the name of Allah, the Most Gracious, the Most Merciful)

الحمد لله ربّ، والصلاة والسلام على نبينا محمد وعلى آله وصحبه أجمعين

All praise is due to Allah, the Lord of all worlds, and may peace and blessings be upon our Prophet Muhammad (peace be upon him) and his family and companions.

Dear brothers and sisters, in this chapter, we will explore the profound healing power of remembrance (Dhikr) and its transformative effects on our emotional and spiritual well-being. Dhikr is a spiritual practice deeply rooted in our Islamic tradition, serving as a means of connecting with Allah and finding solace in His remembrance.

The Importance of Dhikr: Dhikr is a powerful tool that allows us to strengthen our bond with Allah, seek His forgiveness, and

*Sufi Secrets to Inner Healing………..*

find peace amidst the challenges of life. Allah says in the Quran: "Indeed, in the remembrance of Allah do hearts find rest" (Surah Ar-Ra'd, 13:28). This verse emphasizes that true tranquility and inner peace are attained through the remembrance of Allah. Dhikr acts as a soothing balm for our souls, providing comfort and healing to our troubled hearts.

The Prophet Muhammad (peace be upon him) said: "The likeness of the one who remembers his Lord and the one who does not remember Him is like that of the living and the dead" (Sahih Al-Bukhari). This Hadith beautifully illustrates the profound difference between a heart immersed in the remembrance of Allah and a heart devoid of it. Dhikr enlivens our spirits, rejuvenates our faith, and brings us closer to Allah's divine presence.

The Benefits of Dhikr in Healing the Soul: Dhikr has a profound impact on our emotional and spiritual well-being. It serves as a means of seeking forgiveness, dispelling anxiety, and finding solace in times of hardship. Allah says in the Quran: "And

*Sufi Secrets to Inner Healing………..*

remember your Lord within yourself in humility and in fear without being apparent in speech" (Surah Al-A'raf, 7:205). This verse reminds us to engage in inward remembrance, fostering a deep connection with Allah that transcends mere verbal utterance.

The Prophet Muhammad (peace be upon him) said: "There are some hearts that are like mirrors; they derive benefit from everything. And there are other hearts that are like glass; they do not retain anything" (Sunan Ibn Majah). This Hadith highlights the importance of having a receptive heart, capable of absorbing the blessings and wisdom found in the remembrance of Allah. Dhikr purifies our hearts, removes distractions, and allows us to focus on our Creator, thereby healing our souls from the burdens of worldly concerns.

Practices of Dhikr for Emotional and Spiritual Well-being: Dhikr encompasses a wide range of practices, including the recitation of specific phrases, the repetition of Allah's beautiful names, and the recitation of Quranic verses. These practices

*Sufi Secrets to Inner Healing...........*

serve as powerful means of connecting with Allah and experiencing the healing power of His remembrance.

One of the most beloved forms of Dhikr is the recitation of the Tasbih (SubhanAllah, Alhamdulillah, Allahu Akbar). These phrases glorify Allah, express gratitude, and affirm His greatness. When we say "SubhanAllah" (Glory be to Allah), we acknowledge the perfection and greatness of our Creator. This phrase reminds us of Allah's infinite wisdom and His flawless creation. Allah says in the Quran: "And whatever beings there are in the heavens and the earth prostrate to Allah willingly or unwillingly" (Surah Ar-Rad, 13:15). By engaging in the remembrance of Allah, we align ourselves with the natural order of creation and experience a sense of harmony and peace.

"Alhamdulillah" (All praise is due to Allah) is a phrase that expresses gratitude towards our Creator. When we say it, we acknowledge that all blessings and favors come from Allah alone. Allah says in the Quran: "And if you should count the favors of Allah, you could not enumerate them" (Surah Ibrahim,

*Sufi Secrets to Inner Healing...........*

14:34). Through the remembrance of Allah, we cultivate a grateful heart, recognizing His abundant blessings and finding contentment in our lives.

"Allahu Akbar" (Allah is the Greatest) is a phrase that signifies the transcendent nature of Allah's greatness. It serves as a powerful reminder that no matter what challenges we face, Allah's power and mercy are greater than any adversity. Allah says in the Quran: "And Allah is the Greatest, and Allah knows what you do not know" (Surah Al-Baqarah, 2:216). Dhikr elevates our spirits, strengthens our faith, and instills within us the confidence that Allah's help and guidance are always available to us.

In addition to these phrases, the recitation of Quranic verses and the repetition of Allah's beautiful names are also powerful forms of Dhikr. Allah says in the Quran: "And remember the name of your Lord and devote yourself to Him with complete devotion" (Surah Al-Muzzammil, 73:8). By engaging in the recitation and contemplation of the Quran, we immerse ourselves in the words

*Sufi Secrets to Inner Healing...........*

of Allah, seeking guidance, and finding solace in His divine revelation.

Conclusion:

Dear brothers and sisters, the healing power of Dhikr is a gift from Allah to His creation. Through the remembrance of Allah, we find solace, strength, and spiritual nourishment. It is a means by which we can purify our hearts, seek forgiveness, and experience the tranquility that comes from being in constant connection with our Creator.

Let us make Dhikr a regular practice in our lives. Let us remember Allah in our hearts, in our thoughts, and on our tongues. May our Dhikr be sincere, filled with love and reverence for Allah. By engaging in the remembrance of Allah, we will witness the transformative effects it has on our emotional and spiritual well-being, and we will draw closer to the ultimate source of healing and peace.

*Sufi Secrets to Inner Healing…………*

May Allah bless us all with the ability to engage in Dhikr and may He grant us the healing and tranquility that comes from His remembrance. Ameen.

And Allah knows best.

Wa Alaikum Assalam wa Rahmatullahi wa Barakatuhu.

## Section 2.2: Dhikr: A Pathway to Spiritual Connection

Assalamu Alaikum wa Rahmatullahi wa Barakatuhu

Dear brothers and sisters, in this section, we will embark on a journey to explore the profound significance of Dhikr as a pathway to spiritual connection with our Creator. Dhikr, the remembrance of Allah, holds immense spiritual power and serves as a means to deepen our bond with Him, seek His closeness, and experience the beauty of His divine presence.

Allah says in the Quran: "And remember Allah often that you may succeed" (Surah Al-Jumu'ah, 62:10). This verse highlights the importance of Dhikr as a key to attaining success in this life and the Hereafter. When we engage in the remembrance of Allah, we open the doors to His mercy, guidance, and blessings.

The Prophet Muhammad (peace be upon him) emphasized the significance of Dhikr in numerous Hadiths. He said: "The similitude of one who remembers his Lord and one who does not remember Him is like that of the living and the dead" (Sahih Al-Bukhari). This Hadith emphasizes the stark contrast between

*Sufi Secrets to Inner Healing...........*

a heart filled with the remembrance of Allah and a heart devoid of it. Dhikr breathes life into our souls, ignites our spiritual connection, and awakens us from the slumber of heedlessness.

Dhikr serves as a bridge that connects us to Allah, allowing us to experience His presence in our daily lives. It is a way to establish an intimate conversation with our Creator, seeking His forgiveness, guidance, and solace. Allah says in the Quran: "O you who have believed, remember Allah with much remembrance" (Surah Al-Ahzab, 33:41). This verse encourages us to engage in abundant remembrance of Allah, recognizing its transformative impact on our spiritual well-being.

There are various forms of Dhikr that we can incorporate into our lives to strengthen our spiritual connection with Allah. One such form is the repetition of His beautiful names and attributes. Allah says in the Quran: "And to Allah belong the best names, so invoke Him by them" (Surah Al-A'raf, 7:180). By reciting and reflecting upon the names of Allah, we deepen our

*Sufi Secrets to Inner Healing………..*

understanding of His infinite qualities and develop a profound sense of awe and reverence.

Another form of Dhikr is the recitation of Quranic verses. Allah says in the Quran: "Recite, [O Muhammad], what has been revealed to you of the Book and establish prayer. Indeed, prayer prohibits immorality and wrongdoing, and the remembrance of Allah is greater. And Allah knows that which you do" (Surah Al-'Ankabut, 29:45). The recitation of the Quran not only nourishes our souls but also serves as a means of seeking guidance and drawing closer to Allah's words of wisdom and enlightenment.

Furthermore, we can engage in silent or audible supplications, praising Allah, seeking His forgiveness, and expressing our gratitude. The Prophet Muhammad (peace be upon him) said: "The best remembrance is 'La ilaha illallah' (There is no deity worthy of worship except Allah)" (Sunan At-Tirmidhi). This simple yet powerful phrase affirms our faith in the oneness of Allah and strengthens our spiritual connection with Him.

*Sufi Secrets to Inner Healing………..*

Dear brothers and sisters, let us embrace Dhikr as a pathway to spiritual connection. Let us strive to incorporate remembrance of Allah into our daily lives, whether through the repetition of His names, the recitation of Quranic verses, or sincere supplications. May our hearts be filled with the remembrance of Allah, and may this remembrance be a source of tranquility, guidance and blessings in our lives.

When we engage in Dhikr, we enter into a state of mindfulness, focusing our thoughts and intentions solely on Allah. This deepens our connection with Him and brings us closer to the spiritual realm. Allah says in the Quran: "And when My servants ask you concerning Me, indeed I am near. I respond to the invocation of the supplicant when he calls upon Me" (Surah Al-Baqarah, 2:186). Through Dhikr, we open the doors of communication with our Creator, knowing that He is always near and ready to respond to our heartfelt prayers.

Moreover, Dhikr acts as a means of purifying our hearts and seeking forgiveness. Allah says in the Quran: "And those who

*Sufi Secrets to Inner Healing...........*

believe, and whose hearts find rest in the remembrance of Allah. Verily, in the remembrance of Allah do hearts find rest" (Surah Ar-Ra'd, 13:28). Dhikr cleanses our souls from impurities, removes distractions, and allows us to reconnect with our innate spiritual nature. It brings tranquility to our hearts and helps us overcome the burdens of worldly concerns.

The Prophet Muhammad (peace be upon him) encouraged his companions to engage in Dhikr and taught them various supplications to recite. He said: "The best remembrance is La ilaha illallah (There is no deity worthy of worship except Allah), and the best supplication is Alhamdulillah (All praise is due to Allah)" (Sunan At-Tirmidhi). These simple yet profound expressions of faith strengthen our spiritual connection and remind us of our ultimate purpose in life: to worship and submit to Allah alone.

Dear brothers and sisters, let us recognize the immense blessings and spiritual benefits that Dhikr brings into our lives. Let us make it a habit to engage in the remembrance of Allah

*Sufi Secrets to Inner Healing………..*

throughout our day, whether in moments of solitude, during our daily activities, or in congregational gatherings. Dhikr is a powerful tool that elevates our spirituality, nurtures our souls, and deepens our relationship with Allah.

As we embark on this journey of Dhikr, let us remember the words of Allah: "So remember Me; I will remember you. And be grateful to Me and do not deny Me" (Surah Al-Baqarah, 2:152). May our hearts be filled with the remembrance of Allah, may it be a constant source of guidance, solace, and spiritual elevation in our lives. And may Allah bless us with the ability to immerse ourselves in the beauty of Dhikr and experience the profound spiritual connection it brings. Ameen.

And Allah knows best.

Wa allahu ta'ala a

*Sufi Secrets to Inner Healing………..*

## Section 2.3: The Benefits of Dhikr in Healing the Soul.

Bismillahir Rahmanir Rahim (In the name of Allah, the Most Gracious, the Most Merciful)

Dear brothers and sisters, in this section, we will delve into the profound benefits of Dhikr in healing the soul. Dhikr is not merely a ritualistic act, but a spiritual practice that has transformative effects on our inner being. It is a means through which we can find solace, peace, and healing in the remembrance of Allah.

**Purification of the Heart:** Dhikr serves as a powerful tool in purifying our hearts from spiritual diseases and negative emotions. Allah says in the Quran: "Indeed, in the remembrance of Allah do hearts find rest" (Surah Ar-Ra'd, 13:28). When we engage in Dhikr, our hearts are cleansed from impurities, such as arrogance, envy, and hatred, allowing us to cultivate qualities of love, humility, and compassion. It is through the remembrance of Allah that we find tranquility and serenity within ourselves.

*Sufi Secrets to Inner Healing………..*

**Connection with Allah:** Dhikr is a means of establishing a deep and intimate connection with our Creator. Allah says in the Quran: "So remember Me; I will remember you" (Surah Al-Baqarah, 2:152). When we engage in the remembrance of Allah, we draw closer to Him, and He, in turn, showers His mercy and blessings upon us. Through Dhikr, we experience a sense of nearness to Allah, knowing that He is always attentive to our prayers and supplications.

**Protection from Shaytan:** Dhikr acts as a shield against the whispers and temptations of Shaytan (Satan). The Prophet Muhammad (peace be upon him) said: "Verily, the house in which Allah is remembered and the house in which Allah is not remembered are like the living and the dead" (Sahih Muslim). When we engage in the remembrance of Allah, Shaytan finds no foothold in our hearts, as our focus and devotion are directed solely towards our Creator. Dhikr serves as a spiritual armor that safeguards our souls from the influence of evil forces.

*Sufi Secrets to Inner Healing………..*

**Emotional Healing:** Dhikr has a profound impact on our emotional well-being. It provides solace and comfort to the troubled heart. Allah says in the Quran: "Those who have believed and whose hearts are assured by the remembrance of Allah. Unquestionably, by the remembrance of Allah, hearts are assured" (Surah Ar-Ra'd, 13:28). Through Dhikr, we find relief from anxiety, stress, and sadness, as our hearts are enveloped in the divine remembrance of Allah's love, mercy, and guidance.

**Increased Faith and Gratitude:** Dhikr strengthens our faith and nurtures a sense of gratitude within us. The Prophet Muhammad (peace be upon him) said: "Whoever says, 'SubhanAllah wa bihamdihi' (Glory be to Allah and praise Him) a hundred times a day, his sins will be forgiven even if they are like the foam of the sea" (Sahih Al-Bukhari). When we engage in Dhikr, we acknowledge the greatness of Allah and express our gratitude for His countless blessings upon us. This cultivates a deeper appreciation for the blessings in our lives and strengthens our faith in Allah's divine providence.

*Sufi Secrets to Inner Healing………..*

**Spiritual Upliftment:** Dhikr elevates our spirituality and increases our awareness of the divine presence. Allah says in the Quran: "And men who remember Allah often and women who do so – for them Allah has prepared forgiveness and a great reward" (Surah Al-Ahzab, 33:35). Through consistent and sincere Dhikr, our souls are uplifted, and we experience a sense of closeness to Allah. Our hearts become more attuned to His guidance, and we develop a heightened spiritual consciousness. Dhikr allows us to transcend the worldly distractions and focus our attention on the eternal realm, fostering a deeper connection with our Creator.

**Inner Peace and Contentment:** Dhikr brings inner peace and contentment to our souls. Allah says in the Quran: "Indeed, by the remembrance of Allah, hearts are assured" (Surah Ar-Ra'd, 13:28). When we engage in Dhikr, our hearts find tranquility, as we surrender our worries and concerns to Allah. The remembrance of His names and attributes instills in us a sense of trust and reliance on His wisdom and plan for us. Through

Dhikr, we discover a lasting source of peace that transcends the fleeting pleasures of this world.

**Increased Barakah (Blessings):** Dhikr attracts the blessings of Allah into our lives. The Prophet Muhammad (peace be upon him) said: "When a group of people assemble for the remembrance of Allah, the angels surround them, (Allah's) mercy envelops them, tranquility descends upon them, and Allah mentions them to those who are with Him" (Sahih Muslim). When we engage in collective Dhikr, we open the gates for divine blessings to shower upon us. These blessings manifest in various aspects of our lives, including our relationships, health, sustenance, and overall well-being.

**Strengthening of Faith and Taqwa:** Dhikr serves as a means to strengthen our faith and increase our consciousness of Allah (Taqwa). Allah says in the Quran: "O you who have believed, remember Allah with much remembrance" (Surah Al-Ahzab, 33:41). The remembrance of Allah reinforces our faith in His existence, His attributes, and His promise of reward and

*Sufi Secrets to Inner Healing………..*

punishment. It reminds us of our ultimate purpose in life and motivates us to live a life of righteousness, conscious of our actions and their consequences.

Dear brothers and sisters, the benefits of Dhikr are numerous and far-reaching. Through the remembrance of Allah, we find healing, peace, and spiritual elevation. Let us embrace Dhikr as a regular practice in our lives, both individually and collectively. Let us fill our hearts and tongues with the praise and remembrance of Allah, seeking His forgiveness, guidance, and blessings.

**Remember the words of Allah:** "And remember Allah often that you may succeed" (Surah Al-Jumu'ah, 62:10). May our souls be rejuvenated through the power of Dhikr, and may it lead us to a deeper connection with our Creator. May Allah grant us the strength and devotion to engage in abundant remembrance of Him and may He bless us with the immense rewards and benefits that Dhikr entails. Ameen.

And Allah knows best.

*Sufi Secrets to Inner Healing………..*

## Section 2.3: Practices of Dhikr for Emotional and Spiritual Well-being

Bismillahir Rahmanir Rahim

Dear brothers and sisters, in this section, we will go into the practices of Dhikr for emotional and spiritual well-being. Dhikr is a powerful tool that allows us to nourish our souls, find inner peace, and strengthen our connection with Allah. Let us explore some key practices of Dhikr that bring about profound emotional and spiritual benefits.

**Tasbih (SubhanAllah):** One of the most commonly practiced forms of Dhikr is the recitation of "SubhanAllah" (Glory be to Allah). This simple yet profound phrase reminds us of the greatness and perfection of Allah. It acknowledges His infinite attributes and qualities. Allah says in the Quran: "Glorify the name of your Lord, the Most High" (Surah Al-A'la, 87:1). By engaging in the constant recitation of "SubhanAllah," we affirm our belief in Allah's greatness and express our gratitude for His blessings.

*Sufi Secrets to Inner Healing...........*

**Tahleel (La ilaha illallah):** The recitation of "La ilaha illallah" (There is no deity worthy of worship except Allah) is another essential practice of Dhikr. This phrase encapsulates the fundamental principle of Tawheed (Oneness of Allah). Allah says in the Quran: "And know that there is no deity except Allah and ask forgiveness for your sin" (Surah Muhammad, 47:19). The constant remembrance of "La ilaha illallah" reminds us of the unity of Allah and reinforces our commitment to worship Him alone.

**Takbeer (Allahu Akbar):** The recitation of "Allahu Akbar" (Allah is the Greatest) is a powerful form of Dhikr that uplifts our spirits and affirms our faith. It serves as a reminder that Allah is greater than any challenge, difficulty, or worldly possession. Allah says in the Quran: "And Allah is the Greatest, and Allah knows what you do not know" (Surah Al-Baqarah, 2:216). By engaging in the frequent recitation of "Allahu Akbar," we acknowledge Allah's supreme power and seek His guidance and assistance in all aspects of our lives.

*Sufi Secrets to Inner Healing...........*

**Istighfar (Seeking Forgiveness):** Istighfar is an integral part of Dhikr, wherein we seek forgiveness from Allah for our shortcomings and sins. Allah says in the Quran: "And seek forgiveness of your Lord and repent to Him" (Surah Hud, 11:3). Engaging in Istighfar not only purifies our hearts but also brings about emotional relief and spiritual upliftment. It is a means of seeking Allah's mercy and turning back to Him in repentance.

**Salawat (Sending Blessings upon the Prophet):** Sending blessings upon the Prophet Muhammad (peace be upon him), known as Salawat, is a beloved form of Dhikr. It is a means of showing love, respect, and gratitude towards the Messenger of Allah. Allah says in the Quran: "Indeed, Allah confers blessing upon the Prophet, alqnd His angels [ask Him to do so]. O you who have believed, ask [Allah to confer] blessing upon him and ask [Allah to grant him] peace" (Surah Al-Ahzab, 33:56). By frequently reciting Salawat, we not only honor the Prophet but also receive blessings and divine mercy in return.

*Sufi Secrets to Inner Healing...........*

**Quranic Reflection and Recitation:** Engaging in the recitation and contemplation of the Quran is a profound form of Dhikr that nourishes our souls and provides solace to our hearts. Allah says in the Quran: "And We have certainly made the Quran easy for remembrance, so is there anyone who will take heed?" (Quran 54:17)

In this book, we delve into the beauty and significance of Quranic reflection and recitation, exploring the transformative power it holds for our spiritual growth and inner healing. As we immerse ourselves in the divine words, we embark on a journey of self-discovery, seeking wisdom, guidance, and solace in the verses revealed by Allah.

Through clear explanations, practical guidance, and inspiring insights, we unravel the depths of Quranic recitation and its profound impact on our hearts and minds. We explore the art of Tajweed, the rules of proper recitation, and delve into the secrets of reciting the Quran with sincerity and devotion.

*Sufi Secrets to Inner Healing………..*

Drawing upon the teachings of the Prophet Muhammad (peace be upon him), we discover the immense blessings and rewards of engaging with the Quran, both in our daily lives and during special moments of reflection and worship. With the Prophet as our exemplar, we learn how to connect with the Quran on a deeper level, allowing its timeless wisdom to permeate our souls and guide us towards spiritual fulfillment.

Moreover, we explore the practice of Tadabbur, the contemplation of the Quranic verses, as a means of gaining insight, inspiration, and clarity in our lives. Through thought-provoking reflections and practical exercises, we uncover the hidden gems within the Quran, discovering how its teachings can address our individual struggles, heal our wounds, and bring us closer to Allah.

As we embark on this journey of Quranic reflection and recitation, may our hearts be open to the divine guidance, our minds receptive to the profound truths, and our souls nourished by the mercy and love of Allah. May the Quran become a

*Sufi Secrets to Inner Healing...........*

constant companion in our lives, a source of comfort, guidance, and transformation.

With gratitude to Allah and the tireless efforts of the scholars, teachers, and all those who have preserved and transmitted the Quran throughout history, I present this book as a humble contribution to the quest for Quranic understanding and the deepening of our spiritual connection with the divine words. May it inspire and empower you to embark on a lifelong journey of Quranic reflection and recitation, leading to inner peace, spiritual growth, and closeness to Allah.

*Sufi Secrets to Inner Healing…………*

# Chapter Three

## Section 3.1: Purifying the Heart: The Key to Inner Healing.

Bismillahir Rahmanir Rahim (In the name of Allah, the Most Gracious, the Most Merciful).

Dear brothers and sisters, in this chapter, we explore the profound concept of purifying the heart, which is the key to inner healing. Our hearts are the core of our beings, and their purity is essential for our emotional and spiritual well-being. Let us delve into the process of purifying the heart and discover the transformative power it holds.

**Recognizing the Diseases of the Heart:** The first step towards purifying the heart is to recognize and identify the diseases that afflict it. Just as physical ailments require diagnosis for proper treatment, our hearts too need a thorough examination. The Quran describes various diseases of the heart, such as arrogance (Quran 7:146), envy (Quran 113:5), and hypocrisy (Quran 63:4). By introspecting and reflecting upon our thoughts, intentions,

*Sufi Secrets to Inner Healing...........*

and actions, we can identify these diseases and seek their remedy.

**Tazkiyah:** The Art of Purification: Tazkiyah is the process of purifying the heart and elevating its spiritual state. It involves self-reflection, self-discipline, and seeking Allah's guidance and forgiveness. Allah says in the Quran: "Indeed, successful is the one who purifies himself" (Surah Al-A'la, 87:14). Tazkiyah requires sincere efforts to cleanse our hearts from impurities, negative traits, and sinful inclinations. It is a continuous journey of self-improvement and seeking closeness to Allah.

Seeking Repentance: Repentance (Tawbah) is a crucial aspect of purifying the heart. It is a heartfelt acknowledgment of our sins, remorse for our wrongdoings, and a sincere commitment to change. Allah says in the Quran: "And turn to Allah in repentance, all of you, O believers, that you might succeed" (Surah An-Nur, 24:31). By seeking forgiveness from Allah and making a firm resolve to rectify our actions, we cleanse our hearts and open the doors of mercy and forgiveness.

*Sufi Secrets to Inner Healing…………*

**Cultivating Good Character:** Purifying the heart involves cultivating good character traits that reflect the teachings of Islam. The Prophet Muhammad (peace be upon him) said: "The heaviest thing that will be placed in the balance of a believing servant on the Day of Resurrection will be good character" (Sunan At-Tirmidhi). Developing traits such as patience, kindness, humility, and compassion helps purify our hearts and strengthens our connection with Allah and our fellow human beings.

**Reflection on the Quran:** The Quran is a powerful source of guidance and purification for the heart. Allah says in the Quran: "This is a Book about which there is no doubt, a guidance for those conscious of Allah" (Surah Al-Baqarah, 2:2). By engaging in the regular recitation, contemplation, and implementation of the Quran, we allow its transformative message to purify our hearts and guide our actions. The Quran serves as a mirror that reflects the state of our hearts and guides us towards righteousness.

*Sufi Secrets to Inner Healing………..*

**Supplication (Dua):** Making sincere supplications to Allah is a means of purifying the heart and seeking His assistance in the journey of inner healing. Allah says in the Quran: "And your Lord says, 'Call upon Me; I will respond to you'" (Surah Ghafir, 40:60). Through heartfelt prayers, we acknowledge our dependence on Allah, seek His guidance, and ask for His blessings and mercy. Dua is a powerful tool that connects us with our Creator and brings solace and healing to our hearts.

Dear brothers and sisters, purifying the heart is a lifelong endeavor that requires dedication, self-reflection, and seeking Allah's guidance. It is a process that requires constant vigilance and striving for self-improvement. As we embark on this journey of purifying our hearts, let us remember the words of the Prophet Muhammad (peace be upon him) who said: "Indeed, Allah does not look at your outward forms and possessions, but He looks at your hearts and your deeds" (Sahih Muslim).

In our pursuit of inner healing, it is important to remember that purifying the heart goes hand in hand with righteous actions.

*Sufi Secrets to Inner Healing............*

Our actions should align with the teachings of Islam and be motivated by sincerity and a desire to please Allah. The Prophet Muhammad (peace be upon him) said: "Verily, Allah does not look at your faces or your wealth, but He looks at your hearts and your deeds" (Sahih Muslim).

As we strive to purify our hearts, let us seek inspiration from the stories of the Prophets and righteous individuals mentioned in the Quran. Their examples serve as a reminder that inner healing is attainable through steadfastness, faith, and adherence to the teachings of Islam. Allah says in the Quran: "And We have certainly sent messengers before you and assigned to them wives and descendants. And it was not for a messenger to come with a sign except by permission of Allah" (Surah Ar-Ra'd, 13:38).

Brothers and sisters, purifying the heart is not an easy task, but it is a noble and rewarding endeavor. It requires self-reflection, self-discipline, and a sincere intention to please Allah. Remember, Allah is the ultimate healer, and with His guidance

*Sufi Secrets to Inner Healing…………*

and mercy, we can attain a purified heart that brings us closer to Him.

In conclusion, let us strive to purify our hearts by recognizing the diseases that afflict them, engaging in the art of Tazkiyah, seeking repentance, cultivating good character, reflecting on the Quran, and supplicating to Allah. By doing so, we pave the way for inner healing, emotional well-being, and a stronger connection with our Creator. May Allah bless us all with hearts that are pure, and may He grant us the strength and guidance to embark on this transformative journey. Ameen.

"And those who believe and do righteous deeds, their Lord will admit them to His mercy. That is what is the clear attainment" (Surah Al-Jathiya, 45:30).

*Sufi Secrets to Inner Healing………..*

## Section 3.2: Recognizing the Diseases of the Heart
Bismillahir Rahmanir Rahim

Dear brothers and sisters, in Islam, recognizing the diseases of the heart is of utmost importance in our journey towards spiritual growth and inner healing. The diseases of the heart refer to negative traits, attitudes, and behaviors that hinder our connection with Allah and disrupt our emotional well-being. It is crucial for us to identify and understand these diseases so that we can seek their remedy and strive towards a purified heart.

**Arrogance (Kibr):** Arrogance is a destructive disease of the heart that leads to pride, self-importance, and a sense of superiority over others. Allah warns against arrogance in the Quran: "And do not turn your cheek [in contempt] toward people and do not walk through the earth exultantly. Indeed, Allah does not like everyone self-deluded and boastful" (Surah Luqman, 31:18). The Prophet Muhammad (peace be upon him) said: "No one with an atom's weight of arrogance in his heart will enter Paradise" (Sahih Muslim). Recognizing and

*Sufi Secrets to Inner Healing...........*

overcoming arrogance requires humility and recognizing that all blessings and successes come from Allah alone.

**Envy (Hasad):** Envy is a disease that stems from discontentment with the blessings and achievements of others. It leads to feelings of resentment and ill-will towards others. Allah warns against envy in the Quran: "Or do they envy people for what Allah has given them of His bounty? But we had already given the family of Abraham the Scripture and wisdom and conferred upon them a great kingdom" (Surah An-Nisa, 4:54). The Prophet Muhammad (peace be upon him) said: "Beware of envy, for envy consumes good deeds just as fire consumes wood" (Sunan Abu Dawood). Recognizing envy requires cultivating contentment and gratitude for the blessings bestowed upon us by Allah.

**Hypocrisy (Nifaq):** Hypocrisy is a disease of the heart where one outwardly displays faith while inwardly harboring disbelief or insincerity. Allah condemns hypocrisy in the Quran: "When the hypocrites come to you, [O Muhammad], they say, 'We testify that you are the Messenger of Allah.' And Allah knows that you are His Messenger, and Allah testifies that the hypocrites are liars" (Surah Al-Munafiqun, 63:1). The Prophet Muhammad (peace be upon him) said: "The signs of a hypocrite are three: when he speaks, he lies; when he makes a promise, he breaks it; and when he is entrusted with something, he betrays the trust" (Sahih Al-Bukhari). Recognizing hypocrisy requires self-reflection and striving for sincerity in our thoughts, words, and actions.

**Greed (Tama'):** Greed is a disease of the heart characterized by an insatiable desire for wealth, possessions, and worldly pleasures. It leads to selfishness, exploitation, and neglect of others' rights. Allah warns against greed in the Quran: "And let not those who [greedily] withhold what Allah has given them of His bounty ever think that it is better for them. Rather, it is worse for them. Their necks will be encircled by what they withheld on the Day of Resurrection" (Surah Al Imran, 3:180). The Prophet Muhammad (peace be upon him) said: "Beware of greed, for it was greed that destroyed those who came before you" (Sunan Ibn Majah). Recognizing greed requires contentment with what Allah has provided and a focus on the eternal rewards of the hereafter.

Brothers and sisters, recognizing the diseases of the heart is the first step towards their remedy. By identifying these diseases and acknowledging their presence within ourselves, we can seek the necessary measures to rectify them and purify our hearts.

It is essential to remember that Islam provides us with guidance and solutions to combat these diseases. The Quran and Hadiths offer invaluable teachings that help us recognize and address the ailments of our hearts.

One key aspect of recognizing the diseases of the heart is self-reflection. We must take the time to introspect and assess our intentions, thoughts, and actions. Are we motivated by sincerity and seeking the pleasure of Allah, or are there hidden desires and negative traits clouding our hearts?

In Surah Al-Hujurat, Allah says: "Indeed, We have created man and We know what his soul whispers to him, and We are closer

*Sufi Secrets to Inner Healing…………*

to him than [his] jugular vein" (Quran, 50:16). This verse reminds us that Allah is fully aware of our innermost thoughts and inclinations. Therefore, it is crucial for us to be honest with ourselves and acknowledge any diseases that may be present within our hearts.

In addition to self-reflection, seeking knowledge is paramount in recognizing the diseases of the heart. Studying the Quran, reflecting upon its verses, and contemplating the teachings of the Prophet Muhammad (peace be upon him) through Hadiths can provide profound insights into the various diseases that afflict our hearts.

The Prophet Muhammad (peace be upon him) said: "The cure for ignorance is to ask questions." Therefore, let us be proactive in seeking knowledge and understanding the diseases of the heart. Attend religious lectures, read books by reputable scholars, and engage in discussions with knowledgeable individuals to enhance our understanding of these diseases and their remedies.

*Sufi Secrets to Inner Healing………..*

Furthermore, seeking the guidance of Allah through sincere supplication (dua) is crucial in recognizing the diseases of the heart. Allah says in the Quran: "And when My servants ask you concerning Me, indeed, I am near. I respond to the invocation of the supplicant when he calls upon Me" (Quran, 2:186). Turn to Allah in humility and sincerity, seeking His guidance and assistance in recognizing and overcoming the diseases within our hearts.

Brothers and sisters, recognizing the diseases of the heart is not meant to discourage or dishearten us. Instead, it is a call to action, a reminder that we have the ability to rectify our hearts and seek healing through the mercy of Allah.

Let us strive to recognize the diseases of the heart such as arrogance, envy, hypocrisy, and greed. Through self-reflection, seeking knowledge, and supplicating to Allah, we can embark on the journey of purifying our hearts and experiencing inner healing.

*Sufi Secrets to Inner Healing………..*

May Allah grant us the awareness to recognize the diseases of our hearts, the strength to overcome them, and the guidance to purify our hearts for His sake. Ameen.

"And We will surely test you until We make evident those who strive among you [for the cause of Allah] and the patient, and We will test your affairs" (Quran, 47:31).

*Sufi Secrets to Inner Healing............*

## Section 3.3: Tazkiyah: The Art of Purification

Assalamu Alaikum wa Rahmatullahi wa Barakatuhu

Beloved Muslim faithful, in Islam, Tazkiyah is the art of purification, a transformative process that aims to purify the heart, mind, and soul. It is a vital aspect of our spiritual journey, as it allows us to attain closeness to Allah, increase in faith, and attain inner peace and tranquility.

Tazkiyah comes from the Arabic word "zaka," which means purification or growth. It involves cleansing ourselves from negative traits, sinful inclinations, and impurities, while nourishing our hearts with positive qualities and virtues.

The teachings of Islam emphasize the importance of Tazkiyah. Allah says in the Quran, "Indeed, Allah does not change the condition of a people until they change what is in themselves" (Quran, 13:11). This verse highlights that true change and transformation begin from within ourselves.

The Prophet Muhammad (peace be upon him) also emphasized the significance of Tazkiyah. He said in a Hadith, "The best

*Sufi Secrets to Inner Healing...........*

among you are those who have the best character" (Sahih Bukhari). This Hadith underscores the importance of purifying our character and attaining moral excellence through the process of Tazkiyah.

Tazkiyah involves several aspects that contribute to the purification of the heart:

Sincere Repentance (Tawbah): Repentance is the first step towards purification. It involves acknowledging our mistakes, feeling remorseful, and seeking forgiveness from Allah. The Quran states, "And turn to Allah in repentance, all of you, O believers, that you might succeed" (Quran, 24:31). Repentance allows us to cleanse our hearts and seek Allah's mercy and forgiveness.

Observance of the Five Pillars of Islam: The pillars of Islam, including the declaration of faith, prayer, fasting, giving charity, and pilgrimage, are essential acts of worship that contribute to our spiritual purification. They instill discipline, mindfulness,

*Sufi Secrets to Inner Healing*………..

and obedience to Allah's commands, helping us purify our intentions and actions.

Self-Reflection and Accountability: Engaging in self-reflection and holding ourselves accountable is crucial in the process of Tazkiyah. Allah says in the Quran, "O you who have believed, fear Allah. And let every soul look to what it has put forth for tomorrow" (Quran, 59:18). By examining our thoughts, words, and deeds, we can identify areas that need improvement and take steps towards self-improvement.

Seeking Knowledge: Acquiring knowledge of Islam is essential for Tazkiyah. It helps us understand the teachings of Allah and the Prophet Muhammad (peace be upon him), and guides us in leading a righteous and fulfilling life. Allah says in the Quran, "So know, [O Muhammad], that there is no deity except Allah" (Quran, 47:19). Seeking knowledge enables us to purify our beliefs, actions, and intentions.

Regular Supplication and Remembrance of Allah: Engaging in regular supplication (dua) and remembrance (dhikr) of Allah

*Sufi Secrets to Inner Healing............*

strengthens our connection with Him and purifies our hearts. Allah says in the Quran, "And remember Allah often that you may succeed" (Quran, 62:10). Through heartfelt supplication and constant remembrance of Allah, we seek His guidance, forgiveness, and mercy, purifying our hearts in the process.

Beloved Muslim faithful, Tazkiyah is a lifelong journey that requires consistent effort, self-reflection, and reliance on Allah. It is a process through which we strive to purify our hearts from negative traits, develop good character, and attain closeness to our Creator.

Let us embark on this journey of Tazkiyah with sincerity and dedication. Here are some practical steps we can take to engage in the art of purification:

**Cultivate Awareness:** Begin by developing a heightened awareness of your thoughts, emotions, and actions. Reflect upon your daily interactions and identify any negative traits or sinful inclinations that may be present within yourself. This self-

*Sufi Secrets to Inner Healing………..*

awareness is crucial in recognizing areas that need improvement and initiating the process of purification.

**Seek Knowledge and Understanding:** Deepen your knowledge of Islamic teachings through the study of the Quran, Hadith, and the works of reputable scholars. Gain insight into the virtues and values that Islam promotes, and understand the consequences of indulging in negative behaviors. Knowledge equips us with the tools to identify and rectify the diseases of the heart.

**Repentance and Seeking Forgiveness:** Turn to Allah with sincere repentance for any past wrongdoings. Seek His forgiveness and commit to abandoning sinful habits. Allah, in His infinite mercy, promises forgiveness to those who sincerely repent. As Allah says in the Quran, "Say, 'O My servants who have transgressed against themselves [by sinning], do not despair of the mercy of Allah. Indeed, Allah forgives all sins'" (Quran, 39:53).

**Practice Self-Discipline:** Exercise self-discipline in your actions and control over your desires. Resist temptations that

*Sufi Secrets to Inner Healing…………*

may lead to sinful behavior and strive for moderation in all aspects of life. Develop a routine that includes acts of worship, such as regular prayer, fasting, and giving charity, as these acts strengthen our resolve and help purify our hearts.

**Engage in Dhikr and Supplication:** Dedicate time each day to engage in the remembrance of Allah (dhikr) and heartfelt supplication (dua). Recite the beautiful names of Allah and reflect upon their meanings. Remember that Allah is always near, ready to respond to the call of the sincere believer. Engaging in dhikr and dua allows us to connect with Allah and seek His guidance and blessings.

**Surround Yourself with Righteous Companions:** Choose your companions wisely and seek the company of those who encourage and inspire you in your pursuit of spiritual purification. Surrounding yourself with righteous individuals who share similar goals will provide a supportive environment for personal growth and development.

**Show Kindness and Compassion:** Embrace the virtues of kindness, compassion, and forgiveness in your interactions with others. Treat people with respect and strive to forgive those who have wronged you. By cultivating these qualities, you not only purify your own heart but also contribute to a more harmonious and compassionate society.

Beloved Muslim faithful, the path of Tazkiyah is a continuous journey of self-improvement and spiritual growth. It requires sincere intention, consistent effort, and reliance on Allah's guidance. As we strive to purify our hearts, let us remember the words of the Prophet Muhammad (peace be upon him): "Verily, Allah does not look at your appearance or wealth but rather He looks at your hearts and actions" (Sahih Muslim).

May Allah bless us with the strength and determination to purify our hearts and grant us the rewards of inner peace, contentment, and closeness to Him. Ameen.

## Section 3.4: The Virtues and Remedies for a Pure Heart

Assalamu Alaikum wa Rahmatullahi wa Barakatuhu

Beloved Muslim faithful, the virtues and remedies for a pure heart are integral aspects of our spiritual journey in Islam. A pure heart is one that is free from negative traits, adorned with virtues, and deeply connected to Allah. It is a heart that is filled with love, compassion, and sincerity towards Allah and His creation. In this section, I will elucidate upon the teachings of Islam regarding the virtues to cultivate and the remedies to purify our hearts.

**Sincerity (Ikhlas):** The foundation of a pure heart lies in sincerity. Allah says in the Quran, "And they were not commanded except to worship Allah, [being] sincere to Him in religion" (Quran, 98:5). Sincerity entails worshiping Allah alone, seeking His pleasure, and purifying our intentions from any form of ostentation or showing off. It is a constant reminder that our actions and worship should solely be for the sake of Allah, without seeking any worldly recognition or praise.

*Sufi Secrets to Inner Healing………..*

**Love for Allah:** Developing a deep and profound love for Allah is a cornerstone of a pure heart. Allah says in the Quran, "And those who believe are stronger in love for Allah" (Quran, 2:165). This love encompasses reverence, gratitude, and devotion towards our Creator. It involves acknowledging Allah's blessings, seeking His nearness, and yearning to please Him in all aspects of our lives.

**Fear of Allah:** Reverential fear of Allah serves as a protective shield for our hearts. It is an awareness that Allah is All-Seeing and All-Knowing, and that we will be held accountable for our actions. Allah says in the Quran, "So fear Allah as much as you are able" (Quran, 64:16). This fear instills consciousness and caution in our behavior, preventing us from engaging in sinful acts and encouraging us to seek forgiveness when we falter.

**Gratitude (Shukr):** Expressing gratitude to Allah is a means of purifying the heart and attracting His blessings. Allah says in the Quran, "And [remember] when your Lord proclaimed, 'If you are grateful, I will surely increase you [in favor]; but if you deny, indeed, My punishment is severe'" (Quran, 14:7). Gratitude involves recognizing and acknowledging Allah's countless blessings in our lives, both big and small, and responding with humility and thankfulness.

**Patience (Sabr):** Patience is an essential virtue in purifying the heart. It is the ability to remain steadfast in the face of trials and tribulations. Allah says in the Quran, "And seek help through patience and prayer, and indeed, it is difficult except for the humbly submissive [to Allah]" (Quran, 2:45). Practicing patience in times of hardship and adversity allows us to develop resilience, trust in Allah's plan, and a deeper connection with Him.

**Forgiveness:** Forgiveness is a powerful remedy for purifying the heart. It involves letting go of grudges, resentments, and grievances, and seeking Allah's forgiveness for our own shortcomings. Allah says in the Quran, "Pardon them and overlook [their misdeeds]. Indeed, Allah loves the doers of good" (Quran, 5:13). By forgiving others and seeking

*Sufi Secrets to Inner Healing............*

forgiveness ourselves, we lighten the burden on our hearts and open the door to Allah's mercy and blessings.

**Seeking Knowledge:** Seeking knowledge is a transformative remedy for purifying the heart. It involves deepening our understanding of Islam and its teachings. Allah says in the Quran, "Indeed, those who fear Allah among His servants are those who have knowledge" (Quran, 35:28

Beloved Muslim faithful, seeking knowledge allows us to acquire a comprehensive understanding of Allah's commandments, His attributes, and the guidance provided by the Prophet Muhammad (peace be upon him). It enables us to distinguish between right and wrong, make informed decisions, and strive for spiritual excellence.

**Remembrance of Allah (Dhikr):** The remembrance of Allah is a powerful tool for purifying the heart. Engaging in dhikr, the repetition of Allah's names and praises, strengthens our connection with Him and brings tranquility to our souls. Allah says in the Quran, "Those who have believed and whose hearts

*Sufi Secrets to Inner Healing...........*

are assured by the remembrance of Allah. Unquestionably, by the remembrance of Allah, hearts are assured" (Quran, 13:28).

**Prayers and Supplications:** Establishing regular prayers (Salah) and engaging in heartfelt supplications (dua) are acts of worship that cleanse and purify our hearts. Through Salah, we humble ourselves before Allah, seeking His guidance and forgiveness. Allah says in the Quran, "Indeed, prayer prohibits immorality and wrongdoing" (Quran, 29:45). Additionally, supplications provide us with a direct means of communication with Allah, allowing us to express our needs, hopes, and aspirations.

**Charity and Generosity:** Acts of charity and generosity hold immense virtues in Islam. They purify the heart by cultivating selflessness, compassion, and empathy towards others. Allah says in the Quran, "And they give food in spite of love for it to the needy, the orphan, and the captive, [saying], 'We feed you only for the countenance of Allah. We wish not from you reward or gratitude'" (Quran, 76:8-9).

*Sufi Secrets to Inner Healing...........*

Beloved Muslim faithful, purifying our hearts is a continuous process that requires self-reflection, self-discipline, and sincere devotion to Allah. It is a journey of self-improvement that ultimately leads to inner peace, contentment, and a closer relationship with our Creator. Let us strive to embody these virtues and remedies in our daily lives, seeking Allah's guidance and blessings every step of the way.

May Allah bless us all with hearts that are pure, illuminated, and filled with His love and mercy. May He grant us the strength to uphold these teachings and reap the abundant rewards they entail. Ameen.

*Sufi Secrets to Inner Healing............*

## Chapter Four

### Section 4.1: Unveiling the Beloved: Love as the Ultimate Healer.

Beloved Muslim faithful, in Chapter 4, titled "Unveiling the Beloved: Love as the Ultimate Healer," we delve into the profound teachings of Islam regarding the transformative power of love. As an Islamic scholar and seasoned preacher, I have witnessed firsthand the extraordinary impact that love can have on our spiritual well-being and inner healing. Allow me to guide you through this journey of understanding and embracing the significance of love in Islam.

**Divine Love:** At the core of Islam lies the concept of divine love, the love between the Creator and His creation. Allah's love for us is boundless and eternal. Allah says in the Quran, "And He is the Forgiving, the Affectionate" (Quran, 85:14). This divine love is a source of comfort, solace, and healing for our hearts. It is an invitation to develop a deep and intimate

*Sufi Secrets to Inner Healing………..*

connection with Allah, knowing that He is the ultimate source of love and compassion.

**Love for Allah:** Islam teaches us to cultivate a profound love for Allah. This love should surpass any worldly attachments or desires. The Prophet Muhammad (peace be upon him) said, "None of you truly believes until I am more beloved to him than his father, his children, and all of mankind" (Sahih Bukhari). Loving Allah entails obedience, devotion, and seeking His pleasure above all else. It is a love that encompasses trust, gratitude, and complete surrender to His will.

**Love for the Prophet Muhammad (peace be upon him):** As Muslims, we are commanded to love and honor the Prophet Muhammad (peace be upon him). His life, teachings, and character serve as a guiding light for us all. Allah says in the Quran, "Say, [O Muhammad], 'If you should love Allah, then follow me, [so] Allah will love you'" (Quran, 3:31). Loving the Prophet Muhammad (peace be upon him) means emulating his noble qualities, spreading his message of peace and compassion, and holding him dear to our hearts.

**Love for fellow human beings:** Islam emphasizes the importance of love and compassion towards our fellow human beings. Allah says in the Quran, "And do good; indeed, Allah loves the doers of good" (Quran, 2:195). This love extends to all humanity, irrespective of their background, race, or beliefs. It is a love that seeks to alleviate the suffering of others, extend a helping hand, and treat others with kindness and respect.

**Self-Love in Islam:** Islam teaches us to cultivate self-love in a balanced and healthy manner. This involves taking care of our physical, emotional, and spiritual well-being. The Prophet Muhammad (peace be upon him) said, "None of you will have faith until he loves for his brother what he loves for himself" (Sahih Muslim). Self-love in Islam encompasses self-respect, self-improvement, and self-care, while being mindful of the rights and well-being of others.

The Healing Power of Love: Love is a profound healer of the heart and soul. It brings solace in times of distress, strengthens our faith, and instills a sense of purpose and meaning in our lives. The Quran affirms this healing power of love when Allah says, "And of His signs is that He created for you from yourselves mates that you may find tranquility in them; and He placed between you affection and mercy" (Quran, 30:21). Love nurtures emotional well-being, fosters harmonious relationships, and allows us to experience the beauty of Allah's creation.

Beloved Muslim faithful, love is a divine gift bestowed upon us by Allah. It is a means of healing and spiritual growth. As an Islamic scholar and seasoned preacher, I have witnessed the profound impact of love in the lives of believers.

**Expressions of Love:** Islam encourages us to express our love for Allah and His creation through various acts of worship and kindness. We can demonstrate our love for Allah by performing prayers with devotion, reciting His names and praises, and engaging in voluntary acts of worship such as fasting and giving

*Sufi Secrets to Inner Healing………..*

charity. Moreover, showing love and compassion towards our fellow human beings through acts of kindness, forgiveness, and generosity is a manifestation of our love for Allah. The Prophet Muhammad (peace be upon him) said, "None of you will truly believe until you love for your brother what you love for yourself" (Sahih Bukhari).

**Love in Relationships:** Islam places great emphasis on cultivating love and compassion within our relationships, be it with our spouses, parents, children, or friends. A healthy and loving family environment is essential for emotional well-being and spiritual growth. The Quran instructs spouses to love and cherish one another, stating, "And of His signs is that He created for you from yourselves mates that you may find tranquility in them; and He placed between you affection and mercy" (Quran, 30:21). Love within the family unit fosters unity, harmony, and a sense of belonging.

**Love and Forgiveness:** Islam teaches us the importance of forgiveness as an expression of love. It is through forgiveness

*Sufi Secrets to Inner Healing...........*

that we release resentment and negativity from our hearts, allowing love to flourish. Allah says in the Quran, "Show forgiveness, enjoin what is good, and turn away from the ignorant" (Quran, 7:199). The Prophet Muhammad (peace be upon him) also emphasized forgiveness, stating, "The strong is not the one who overcomes the people by his strength, but the strong is the one who controls himself while in anger" (Sahih Bukhari). Forgiveness is a powerful act of love that leads to emotional healing and reconciliation.

**Love for the Sake of Allah:** Islam teaches us the concept of "love for the sake of Allah." This means loving and befriending others purely for the pleasure of Allah, without any ulterior motives. Allah says in the Quran, "And those who believed, love Allah more than anything else" (Quran, 2:165). When our love for others is rooted in our love for Allah, it becomes a source of blessing and spiritual growth. The Prophet Muhammad (peace be upon him) said, "There are three qualities whoever has them, will taste the sweetness of faith: to love Allah and His Messenger more than anyone else, to love a person only for the sake of Allah, and to hate returning to disbelief as much as one hates being thrown into the fire" (Sahih Bukhari).

Beloved Muslim faithful, love is a powerful force that has the ability to heal, unite, and elevate our souls. It is a central theme in Islam, emphasizing the importance of love for Allah, the Prophet Muhammad (peace be upon him), our fellow human beings, and ourselves. By embracing love as the ultimate healer, we can experience profound inner transformation, emotional well-being, and spiritual closeness to Allah.

May Allah fill our hearts with pure and sincere love, and may He enable us to express that love in ways that bring joy, harmony, and healing to ourselves and others. Ameen.

## Section 4.2: Divine Love in Islamic Tradition

Assalamu Alaikum wa Rahmatullahi wa Barakatuhu

Respected and Beloved Believers,

Today, I open this page to write as an Islamic scholar and seasoned preacher on the topic: Divine Love in Islamic tradition.

*Sufi Secrets to Inner Healing...........*

As someone who has devoted his life to studying and understanding the teachings of the Holy Quran and the Hadith, I have witnessed the transformative power of Divine Love and its profound impact on the hearts and souls of believers. Allow me to share with you the beauty and significance of this Divine Love, drawing upon the verses of the Quran and the teachings of our beloved Prophet Muhammad (peace be upon him).

My dear brothers and sisters, Divine Love is the foundation upon which our entire relationship with Allah is built. It is a love that surpasses any human comprehension, a love that is boundless and eternal. Allah, in His infinite mercy and compassion, loves His creation unconditionally. The Quran reminds us of this divine love when Allah says, "And He is the Forgiving, the Affectionate" (Quran, 85:14).

Reflect upon this, my dear brothers and sisters. The Creator of the heavens and the earth, the One who holds all power and authority, loves each and every one of us with a love that knows no bounds. He loves us despite our flaws, our mistakes, and our

*Sufi Secrets to Inner Healing………..*

shortcomings. This Divine Love is a source of comfort and solace, a guiding light in times of darkness, and a healing balm for our weary souls.

Allah's love for us is not simply a passive affection; it is an active and continuous expression of care and concern. He is aware of our struggles, our joys, and our sorrows. Allah says in the Quran, "And when My servants ask you concerning Me, indeed I am near. I respond to the invocation of the supplicant when he calls upon Me" (Quran, 2:186). Our Lord is ever ready to listen to our prayers, to answer our supplications, and to shower His blessings upon us.

But Divine Love is not a one-sided affair, my dear brothers and sisters. It requires our sincere devotion, gratitude, and obedience. It calls upon us to strive in His way, to follow His guidance, and to seek His pleasure above all else. The Prophet Muhammad (peace be upon him) said, "If Allah loves a person, He calls Gabriel, saying, 'Allah loves so-and-so, O Gabriel, love him.' So Gabriel would love him and then would make an

*Sufi Secrets to Inner Healing………..*

announcement in the heavens, 'Allah has loved so-and-so, therefore you should love him also'" (Sahih Muslim).

Let us ponder upon this profound Hadith. When Allah loves a person, the entire creation rejoices in that love. Imagine being the recipient of such divine love, my dear brothers and sisters. Our devotion and obedience to Allah become a means of attracting His love, and as a result, we become recipients of love from the heavens and the earth.

Divine Love also demands that we love one another, my dear brothers and sisters. It teaches us to embrace our fellow human beings with compassion, empathy, and kindness. The Prophet Muhammad (peace be upon him) said, "By the One in whose hand is my soul, you will not enter Paradise until you believe, and you will not believe until you love one another" (Sahih Muslim). This love transcends boundaries of race, nationality, and social status. It is a love that encompasses all of humanity, reflecting the unity of our Ummah.

*Sufi Secrets to Inner Healing...........*

Let us strive to be vessels of Divine Love in this world, my dear brothers and sisters. Let us extend a helping hand to those in need, lend a listening ear to those who are suffering, and spread love and compassion wherever we go. Through our words and actions, may

we embody the teachings of Islam and manifest the Divine Love that resides within our hearts.

In the pursuit of Divine Love, we must also recognize that it requires constant effort and self-reflection. We must purify our intentions and strive for excellence in our worship and conduct. Allah says in the Quran, "Say, 'Indeed, my prayer, my rites of sacrifice, my living and my dying are for Allah, Lord of the worlds'" (Quran, 6:162). Our prayers, acts of worship, and even the smallest acts of kindness should be dedicated solely to seeking the pleasure of Allah and strengthening our connection with Him.

Furthermore, Divine Love necessitates a deep understanding and contemplation of the signs of Allah's creation. We are urged to

*Sufi Secrets to Inner Healing...........*

reflect upon the beauty of nature, the intricacies of the human body, and the vastness of the universe. Allah says in the Quran, "Indeed, in the creation of the heavens and the earth and the alternation of the night and the day are signs for those of understanding" (Quran, 3:190). By observing these signs, we deepen our awe and gratitude for the Creator, enhancing our love for Him.

As we continue our journey towards Divine Love, let us not forget the role of repentance and seeking forgiveness. Our beloved Prophet Muhammad (peace be upon him) said, "Allah is more delighted with the repentance of His servant than one of you who is on his camel in a waterless desert, and his camel escapes from him carrying his food and drink. He, having lost hope of finding it, lies down in the shadow of a tree and is overcome with despair, when all of a sudden he finds that his camel has come back to him. He takes hold of its reins and out of boundless joy blurts out, 'O Allah, You are my servant and I am Your Lord!' making a mistake out of extreme delight" (Sahih Muslim).

*Sufi Secrets to Inner Healing............*

This Hadith beautifully illustrates the immense joy and relief Allah feels when a servant sincerely turns to Him in repentance. No matter how distant we may feel from Allah, His mercy is always within reach. By seeking forgiveness and purifying our hearts, we open ourselves to receive an outpouring of Divine Love and mercy.

Beloved Muslim faithful, let us strive to cultivate Divine Love within ourselves and share it with others. Let us remember that Allah's love for us is unconditional, and it is through our devotion, gratitude, and acts of kindness that we draw closer to Him. As we traverse this journey of life, let our hearts be filled with the love of Allah and let us spread that love to all those around us.

May Allah grant us the ability to truly comprehend and experience Divine Love, and may it be a source of healing, comfort, and guidance in our lives. Ameen.

I conclude this sermon with a prayer:

*Sufi Secrets to Inner Healing……….*

O Allah, the Most Merciful and Loving, we beseech You to shower us with Your Divine Love. Grant us the ability to recognize Your signs, to seek Your forgiveness, and to spread love and compassion in the world. Guide us on the path of righteousness and grant us the strength to overcome any obstacles that come in our way. O Allah, unite our hearts in love and grant us the honor of basking in Your Divine Love in this world and the Hereafter. Ameen.

And all praise and thanks are due to Allah, the Lord of all the worlds.

May peace and blessings be upon our beloved Prophet Muhammad, his family, and his companions.

Assalamu Alaikum wa rahmatullahi wa barakatuhu.

*Sufi Secrets to Inner Healing…………*

## Section 4.3: The Role of Love in Spiritual Transformation

Bismillahir Rahmanir Raheem.

All praise and thanks are due to Allah, the Most Compassionate and Merciful. May His peace and blessings be upon our beloved Prophet Muhammad, his family, and his companions.

Dear brothers and sisters in faith,

Today, I pick my paper and pen to write about a profound and transformative aspect of our spiritual journey: the role of love. Love is a force that has the power to ignite our hearts, purify our souls, and guide us towards a deeper connection with Allah. It is through love that we experience spiritual transformation and draw closer to our Creator.

When we speak of love in the context of Islam, it encompasses various dimensions. First and foremost, we must recognize the primacy of our love for Allah. Our love for Him should surpass all other loves in our hearts. Allah says in the Quran, "And of mankind are some who take (for worship) others besides Allah as rivals (to Allah). They love them as they love Allah. But

*Sufi Secrets to Inner Healing............*

those who believe, love Allah more (than anything else)" (Quran, 2:165). This verse reminds us of the need to prioritize our love for Allah above all worldly attachments.

Moreover, our love for Allah should manifest in our obedience to His commandments and the emulation of the exemplary life of our beloved Prophet Muhammad (peace be upon him). The Prophet (pbuh) said, "None of you will have faith till he loves me more than his father, his children, and all mankind" (Sahih al-Bukhari). This Hadith emphasizes the significance of our love for the Prophet (pbuh) and the impact it has on our faith.

Love also extends to our fellow human beings. Allah reminds us in the Quran, "And [yet], among the people are those who take other than Allah as equals [to Him]. They love them as they [should] love Allah. But those who believe are stronger in love for Allah" (Quran, 2:165). Our love for one another as believers should be rooted in the love for the sake of Allah. It is this love that binds us as an ummah and fosters a sense of unity, compassion, and brotherhood.

*Sufi Secrets to Inner Healing………..*

As an Islamic scholar, I have witnessed firsthand the transformative power of love in the lives of individuals. I have seen hearts softened, animosities dissolved, and lives changed through the power of Divine love. Love has the ability to heal wounds, bridge divides, and bring about genuine spiritual growth.

To experience the role of love in our spiritual transformation, we must nurture it through our actions and intentions. Let us strive to cultivate a sincere love for Allah by seeking His pleasure in all that we do. Let us remember the words of the Prophet (pbuh) who said, "The most beloved deeds to Allah are those that are consistent even if they are few" (Sahih al-Bukhari). Consistency in our worship, acts of kindness, and devotion to Allah is a reflection of our love for Him.

Additionally, let us extend love and kindness to our fellow human beings. The Prophet (pbuh) said, "None of you truly believes until he loves for his brother what he loves for himself" (Sahih al-Bukhari). This Hadith emphasizes the importance of empathy, compassion, and selflessness in our interactions with others. By showing love and kindness to one another, we contribute to the betterment of society and pave the way for collective spiritual growth.

Beloved believers, as we reflect upon the role of love in our spiritual transformation, let us remember that love is not merely a sentiment or emotion; it is a profound spiritual state that requires dedication, effort, and sincerity. It is a force that has the potential to elevate us to the highest levels of spiritual attainment.

One of the ways we can nurture and strengthen our love for Allah is through the remembrance of Him. Allah says in the Quran, "Remember Allah with much remembrance" (Quran, 33:41). The remembrance of Allah, known as dhikr, is a powerful means of connecting with Him and deepening our love for Him. Engaging in dhikr regularly, whether through recitation of the Quran, uttering His beautiful names and attributes, or

*Sufi Secrets to Inner Healing...........*

expressing gratitude for His blessings, allows us to maintain a constant awareness of His presence in our lives.

Furthermore, the Prophet Muhammad (pbuh) encouraged us to engage in specific forms of dhikr that hold great spiritual benefits. For example, he said, "The best remembrance is: 'La ilaha illallah' (There is no deity worthy of worship except Allah)" (Sahih al-Bukhari). This simple yet profound declaration serves as a constant reminder of our devotion to Allah and reinforces our love for Him.

In addition to individual acts of remembrance, communal gatherings of dhikr provide a unique opportunity to experience the collective power of love and spirituality. The Prophet (pbuh) said, "When a group of people assemble for the remembrance of Allah, the angels surround them, mercy covers them, tranquility descends upon them, and Allah mentions them to those who are with Him" (Sahih Muslim). Such gatherings serve as a source of inspiration, rejuvenation, and spiritual upliftment, as the hearts of the believers unite in love and devotion to Allah.

*Sufi Secrets to Inner Healing…………*

As we embark on the path of love and spiritual transformation, it is essential to remember that our actions should align with the teachings of Islam. Love should not be divorced from righteousness and obedience to Allah's commands. Allah says in the Quran, "Say, [O Muhammad], 'If you should love Allah, then follow me, [so] Allah will love you and forgive you your sins. And Allah is Forgiving and Merciful'" (Quran, 3:31). True love for Allah necessitates following the guidance of the Prophet (pbuh) and embodying the values and principles of Islam in our daily lives.

Beloved believers, as we conclude this sermon on the role of love in spiritual transformation, let us reflect upon the profound impact love has on our relationship with Allah and our fellow human beings. Let us strive to cultivate a deep and sincere love for Allah, as it is through this love that we find solace, guidance, and ultimate fulfillment. May our hearts be filled with the pure love that leads us to righteousness, compassion, and unity.

*Sufi Secrets to Inner Healing...........*

I pray that Allah blesses each and every one of you with an abundance of His love, mercy, and grace. May He grant us the strength and sincerity to walk the path of love and spiritual transformation, and may our lives be a testament to the power of Divine love.

And Allah knows best.

## Section 4.3: The Manifestations of Love in Sufi Poetry and Literature

Assalamu Alaikum wa Rahmatullahi wa Barakatuhu

Respected brothers and sisters in faith,

I turn this page today to reflect upon the profound manifestations of love in Sufi poetry and literature. As an Islamic scholar and servant of Allah, I have delved deep into the rich heritage of Sufi tradition, and I am honored to share with you the beauty and wisdom that emanates from this sacred realm.

Sufi poetry and literature, with its enchanting verses and profound symbolism, serves as a bridge between the human soul and the Divine. It is a means through which the seekers of truth express their deepest yearnings, joys, and struggles in their journey towards Allah. The verses penned by renowned Sufi masters are like spiritual gems that illuminate the path of love and offer solace to the seeking hearts.

*Sufi Secrets to Inner Healing...........*

In the Quran, Allah, the Most Merciful, states, "And We have already created man and We know what his soul whispers to him, and We are closer to him than [his] jugular vein" (Quran, 50:16). This verse reminds us of Allah's intimate knowledge of our innermost thoughts and desires. Sufi poetry reflects this profound connection between the human soul and the Divine, allowing us to explore the depths of our emotions and experiences through the language of love.

One of the greatest Sufi poets, Rumi, beautifully captures the essence of love in his verses. His poetry speaks to the heart, resonating with the divine longing within us. Rumi once wrote, "Your task is not to seek for love, but merely to seek and find all the barriers within yourself that you have built against it." These words remind us that love is inherent within us, and it is our own limitations and barriers that obstruct its manifestation. Through introspection and self-reflection, we can break down these barriers and allow the light of love to flow freely.

*Sufi Secrets to Inner Healing...........*

Sufi literature also emphasizes the concept of divine love as the ultimate purpose of our existence. Allah says in the Quran, "And they will say, 'Praise to Allah, who has guided us to this; and we would never have been guided if Allah had not guided us'" (Quran, 7:43). The Sufi poets invite us to embark on a transformative journey of love, where every step draws us closer to our Creator. They teach us to seek Allah's pleasure above all else, to surrender our egos, and to immerse ourselves in the ocean of divine love.

Personal experience has taught me the profound impact that Sufi poetry and literature can have on the human soul. It has the power to awaken dormant love, ignite the flame of devotion, and inspire us to seek the Divine in every moment of our lives. The verses of Sufi poets like Rumi, Hafiz, and Ibn Arabi have guided countless seekers throughout the ages, serving as a spiritual compass in their quest for enlightenment and closeness to Allah.

Beloved seekers of truth, let us embrace the rich heritage of Sufi poetry and literature as a means of connecting with our Creator.

*Sufi Secrets to Inner Healing………..*

Let us immerse ourselves in the verses that touch our hearts and stir our souls. As we delve into the ocean of Sufi wisdom, let us remember that love is the essence of our existence and the path that leads us to Allah's eternal pleasure.

May Allah, the Most Loving and Merciful, grant us the ability to recognize and experience His divine love in every aspect of our lives. May He bless us with hearts that are receptive to the messages of love conveyed through Sufi poetry and literature. And may our journey of love and spiritual growth be filled with peace, enlightenment, and the ultimate union with our Beloved.

And Allah knows best.

*Sufi Secrets to Inner Healing…………*

# Chapter Five

## Section 5.1: The Inner Journey of Self-Reflection and Self-Knowledge.

Assalamu Alaikum wa Rahmatullahi wa Barakatuhu

I pick my paper and pen to write to you about the profound chapter of our spiritual journey, Chapter 5: The Inner Journey of Self-Reflection and Self-Knowledge. This chapter holds immense significance in our quest for spiritual growth and self-realization. As an Islamic scholar who has devoted my life to studying the Holy Quran and the teachings of our beloved Prophet Muhammad (peace be upon him), I feel honored to share with you the wisdom and guidance that lies within this sacred chapter.

In the Quran, Allah, the Most Wise, says, "Indeed, Allah will not change the condition of a people until they change what is in themselves" (Quran, 13:11). This verse emphasizes the importance of self-reflection and self-transformation as fundamental aspects of our spiritual journey. It is through

*Sufi Secrets to Inner Healing...........*

introspection and self-awareness that we can identify our shortcomings, purify our hearts, and strive towards becoming the best versions of ourselves.

Self-reflection is a process of turning inward and examining our thoughts, actions, and intentions in light of the guidance of Allah and the teachings of our Prophet Muhammad (peace be upon him). It is a journey of self-discovery, where we seek to understand the depths of our souls and align our lives with the principles of Islam. By critically evaluating ourselves, we can identify areas for improvement and embark on the path of positive change.

The Prophet Muhammad (peace be upon him) beautifully encapsulated the essence of self-reflection when he said, "Whoever knows himself knows his Lord." This profound Hadith reminds us that self-knowledge is intricately connected to our understanding of our Creator. As we delve deeper into our own hearts, we develop a greater awareness of Allah's presence

*Sufi Secrets to Inner Healing............*

within us and recognize the divine attributes that we are called to embody.

Self-reflection also allows us to recognize and rectify our spiritual diseases. Just as physical illnesses require diagnosis and treatment, our souls require constant evaluation and healing. The Quran describes various spiritual diseases that can afflict our hearts, such as arrogance, envy, greed, and hatred. Allah says, "And We will surely test you until We make evident those who strive among you [for the cause of Allah] and the patient, and We will test your affairs" (Quran, 47:31). Through self-reflection, we can identify these diseases and seek the prescribed remedies found in the teachings of Islam.

I speak from personal experience when I say that self-reflection is a transformative process. It requires courage and sincerity to confront our flaws and weaknesses, but the rewards are immense. By acknowledging our shortcomings and seeking forgiveness from Allah, we open the door to spiritual growth and self-improvement. The more we invest in self-reflection, the

*Sufi Secrets to Inner Healing...........*

closer we draw to our Creator, and the greater our capacity to serve Him and His creation.

Beloved members of the congregation, let us embrace the inner journey of self-reflection and self-knowledge with open hearts and sincere intentions. Let us carve out moments of solitude and contemplation to connect with our souls and seek Allah's guidance. As we evaluate ourselves, let us remember the words of the Prophet Muhammad (peace be upon him), "Take account of yourselves before you are taken to account, and weigh your deeds before they are weighed for you."

May Allah, the Most Merciful, bless us with the strength and sincerity to embark on this inner journey of self-reflection. May He grant us the wisdom to recognize our flaws and the determination to rectify them. And may our pursuit of self-knowledge lead us to a deeper connection with Allah, resulting in a life filled with peace, purpose, and righteousness.

And Allah knows best.

*Sufi Secrets to Inner Healing………..*

## Section 5.2: the Self-Exploration in the Light of Islamic Teachings

Assalamu Alaikum wa Rahmatullahi wa Barakatuhu

Respected members of the Islam faith,

I continue my paper and pen work to write about the self-exploration in the light of Islamic teachings. It is a subject that holds great significance in our spiritual journey and offers us a pathway to deep self-awareness and personal growth. As an Islamic scholar who has devoted my life to studying the Holy Quran and the teachings of our beloved Prophet Muhammad (peace be upon him), I feel humbled and honored to share with you the wisdom and guidance that lies within our faith.

In Islam, self-exploration is not merely an individualistic pursuit but a means to draw closer to our Creator and fulfill our purpose in this world. Allah, the Most Wise, says in the Quran, "We will show them Our signs in the horizons and within themselves until it becomes clear to them that it is the truth" (Quran, 41:53). These divine signs within ourselves serve as a reminder of the infinite wisdom and beauty of Allah's creation.

*Sufi Secrets to Inner Healing………..*

Self-exploration involves delving deep into our hearts and minds, seeking a greater understanding of our thoughts, emotions, and aspirations. It is a journey of introspection and self-discovery, where we strive to align our lives with the teachings of Islam and uncover the unique talents and potentials that Allah has bestowed upon us.

One of the fundamental aspects of self-exploration is the recognition of our purpose in life. Allah says in the Quran, "I did not create the jinn and mankind except to worship Me" (Quran, 51:56). Each one of us has a unique role to play in this world, and it is through self-exploration that we can uncover our true calling and contribute meaningfully to society. By reflecting on our strengths, passions, and values, we can align our actions with our purpose and find fulfillment in serving Allah and His creation.

Self-exploration also involves assessing our character and striving for self-improvement. The Prophet Muhammad (peace be upon him) emphasized the importance of introspection when

*Sufi Secrets to Inner Healing………..*

he said, "The best of you is the one who is best to his family, and I am the best of you to my family." This Hadith teaches us that true righteousness begins with self-reflection and extends to our interactions with others. By examining our conduct and seeking to embody the noble qualities taught by our faith, we can become better individuals and contribute positively to our families, communities, and the world at large.

Furthermore, self-exploration requires us to confront our weaknesses and seek forgiveness and guidance from Allah. The Quran reminds us, "And when My servants ask you concerning Me, indeed I am near. I respond to the invocation of the supplicant when he calls upon Me" (Quran, 2:186). Through sincere supplication and seeking forgiveness, we acknowledge our shortcomings and open ourselves to the divine mercy and guidance of Allah. It is through this process that we can experience personal transformation and spiritual growth.

My beloved brothers and sisters, self-exploration is a continuous and lifelong journey. It requires patience, perseverance, and an unwavering commitment to seeking knowledge and understanding. As an Islamic scholar and seasoned preacher, I can attest to the transformative power of self-exploration. By striving to know ourselves better, we can cultivate a deep sense of gratitude for the blessings bestowed upon us, and we can utilize our unique gifts to serve Allah and uplift humanity.

I urge each and every one of you to embark on this journey of self-exploration with sincerity and an open heart. Set aside moments of solitude and reflection, engage in self-assessment, and seek guidance from the Quran and the teachings of our beloved Prophet (peace be upon him). Allah promises in the Quran, "And those who strive in Our cause - We will surely guide them to Our ways. And indeed, Allah is with the doers of good" (Quran, 29:69). Therefore, have faith that as you embark on the path of self-exploration, Allah will guide you and shower you with His blessings.

During your journey of self-exploration, you may encounter challenges and face moments of self-doubt. Remember that

*Sufi Secrets to Inner Healing*...........

these struggles are an inherent part of the process. The Prophet Muhammad (peace be upon him) said, "The greater the struggle, the greater the reward." Embrace the difficulties as opportunities for growth and trust in Allah's plan for you.

As you delve deeper into self-exploration, I encourage you to engage in practices that promote self-reflection and self-awareness. Make time for daily contemplation, where you assess your thoughts, actions, and intentions. Engage in heartfelt supplication and seek forgiveness for your mistakes. Establish a habit of journaling, as it allows you to express your thoughts and emotions, providing clarity and insight into your innermost self.

Additionally, seek guidance from the teachings of our beloved Prophet Muhammad (peace be upon him). His life serves as a remarkable example of self-exploration and spiritual growth. Study his character, his interactions with others, and his devotion to Allah. In his teachings, you will find profound wisdom and guidance that can aid you in your own journey of self-discovery.

*Sufi Secrets to Inner Healing………..*

Furthermore, connect with fellow believers who share your passion for self-exploration. Surround yourself with individuals who encourage and support your spiritual growth. Together, you can engage in discussions, share insights, and provide mutual encouragement on this sacred path.

Always remember that self-exploration is not a selfish pursuit. As you delve deeper into understanding yourself, you become better equipped to fulfill your responsibilities towards your family, community, and society at large. The knowledge you gain from self-exploration empowers you to make positive contributions and positively impact the lives of those around you.

In conclusion, my dear brothers and sisters, the journey of self-exploration in the light of Islamic teachings is a transformative and rewarding endeavor. Through self-reflection, seeking knowledge, and connecting with Allah, you will discover the depth of your own soul and uncover the immense potential that

*Sufi Secrets to Inner Healing...........*

lies within you. Trust in Allah's guidance, be patient with yourself, and remain steadfast in your pursuit of self-discovery.

May Allah bless each one of you on your journey of self-exploration and grant you the strength, wisdom, and clarity to know yourselves and to live a life that is pleasing to Him. May He fill your hearts with His love and mercy, and may your journey lead you closer to Him in every moment of your life. Ameen.

Peace be upon you all.

## Section 5.3: The Significance of Self-Awareness on the Spiritual Path

Assalamu Alaikum wa Rahmatullahi wa Barakatuhu

In this section, I wish to delve into a topic of great significance on the spiritual path - the importance of self-awareness. In the pursuit of our spiritual journey, self-awareness serves as a guiding light, illuminating our hearts and minds, and leading us closer to the Divine presence.

Allah, in His infinite wisdom, reminds us in the Quran, "Indeed, Allah will not change the condition of a people until they change what is in themselves" (Quran, 13:11). This verse beautifully encapsulates the essence of self-awareness. It emphasizes that our transformation and growth begin with self-reflection and self-awareness. We must acknowledge our strengths and weaknesses, recognize our flaws, and strive for self-improvement.

Self-awareness helps us recognize the true nature of our thoughts, intentions, and actions. It allows us to examine our relationship with Allah and assess whether we are truly aligning

*Sufi Secrets to Inner Healing*...........

ourselves with His teachings. It enables us to identify the barriers that hinder our spiritual growth and guides us towards overcoming them.

In the words of the Prophet Muhammad (peace be upon him), "He who knows himself knows his Lord." This profound Hadith emphasizes the intimate connection between self-awareness and our relationship with Allah. By knowing ourselves, we gain a deeper understanding of our Creator, His attributes, and His guidance. Self-awareness enables us to reflect on our purpose in life, our moral compass, and our responsibility towards ourselves and others.

To cultivate self-awareness, we must engage in introspection and self-examination. Take moments of solitude to ponder upon your thoughts, actions, and emotions. Ask yourself: Am I living in accordance with the teachings of Islam? Am I striving to purify my heart and soul? Am I treating others with kindness and compassion?

*Sufi Secrets to Inner Healing………..*

The Quran provides us with numerous verses that encourage self-reflection and self-awareness. Allah says, "O you who have believed, fear Allah. And let every soul look to what it has put forth for tomorrow" (Quran, 59:18). This verse reminds us of the importance of taking account of our actions and their consequences. By being conscious of our choices, we can ensure that we are making decisions that are in line with our faith and beneficial for our spiritual growth.

Self-awareness also enables us to develop a deeper connection with our fellow human beings. When we are aware of our own strengths and weaknesses, we become more empathetic and understanding towards others. We recognize that we are all flawed beings on a journey of self-improvement, and we treat others with compassion, forgiveness, and humility.

In my own personal experience as an Islamic scholar and preacher, I have witnessed the transformative power of self-awareness. It has allowed me to recognize my own shortcomings, seek forgiveness from Allah, and strive towards

*Sufi Secrets to Inner Healing*…………

personal growth. It has enabled me to connect with others on a deeper level, understanding their struggles and offering support and guidance.

My beloved brothers and sisters, let us not underestimate the significance of self-awareness on our spiritual path. Let us make a conscious effort to examine ourselves, to purify our intentions, and to align our actions with the teachings of Islam. Let us strive for self-improvement, seeking Allah's guidance and forgiveness along the way.

Remember, self-awareness is not a destination but a continuous journey. It requires patience, self-reflection, and constant effort. But the rewards are immeasurable. As we develop self-awareness, we will find ourselves drawing closer to Allah, experiencing inner peace, and becoming the best versions of ourselves.

May Allah bless each one of you with the gift of self-awareness and guide you on your spiritual journey. May He grant you the strength and wisdom to delve deep into your hearts, to introspect

*Sufi Secrets to Inner Healing............*

and reflect upon your actions, and to seek His guidance in all aspects of your life.

In this journey of self-awareness, let us turn to the Quran, the ultimate source of divine guidance. Allah says, "And [mention] when your Lord took from the children of Adam - from their loins - their descendants and made them testify of themselves, [saying to them], 'Am I not your Lord?' They said, 'Yes, we have testified'" (Quran, 7:172). This verse reminds us of the primordial covenant we made with Allah, acknowledging Him as our Lord. It invites us to revisit that covenant, to recognize our ultimate purpose, and to align our lives with His divine will.

Self-awareness requires us to engage in sincere self-assessment. We must scrutinize our intentions, seeking to purify them for the sake of Allah alone. As the Prophet Muhammad (peace be upon him) taught us, "Actions are judged by intentions." Let us constantly examine our motives, ensuring that our deeds are driven by a genuine desire to please Allah and attain His pleasure.

*Sufi Secrets to Inner Healing………..*

The path of self-awareness also entails acknowledging and rectifying our spiritual ailments. We must identify the diseases of the heart, such as arrogance, envy, and greed, and strive to overcome them. The Prophet Muhammad (peace be upon him) said, "Beware of envy, for envy consumes good deeds just as fire consumes wood." This Hadith warns us against the destructive nature of envy and reminds us to cultivate contentment and gratitude.

Self-awareness also necessitates accountability for our words and actions. We must reflect upon the impact our behavior has on ourselves and those around us. Allah says, "Not a word does he (or she) utter, but there is a watcher by him (or her) ready (to record it)" (Quran, 50:18). Let us be mindful of our speech, ensuring that it is filled with kindness, honesty, and compassion.

Furthermore, self-awareness encompasses seeking forgiveness and repentance. We are all prone to mistakes and lapses in judgment. However, it is through sincere repentance that we can seek Allah's forgiveness and strive for self-improvement. Allah

*Sufi Secrets to Inner Healing………..*

says, "And turn to Allah in repentance, all of you, O believers, that you might succeed" (Quran, 24:31). Let us humbly turn to Allah, acknowledging our faults and seeking His mercy and forgiveness.

Finally, self-awareness leads us to the path of continuous self-growth and self-development. As we strive to know ourselves better, we also deepen our understanding of Allah's infinite mercy and love for His creation. It is through this journey that we come to appreciate the blessings bestowed upon us and utilize them in the service of humanity.

My dear brothers and sisters, the path of self-awareness is not an easy one, but it is a transformative one. It requires courage, humility, and a sincere desire for self-improvement. As an Islamic scholar and preacher, I have personally experienced the power of self-awareness in my own spiritual journey. It has allowed me to recognize my weaknesses, seek forgiveness, and strive for personal growth. It has strengthened my connection with Allah and enriched my relationships with others.

*Sufi Secrets to Inner Healing...........*

I invite you all to embark on this journey of self-awareness. Reflect upon your actions, intentions, and character. Seek the guidance of Allah through His words in the Quran and the teachings of the Prophet Muhammad (peace be upon him). Embrace the process of self-discovery, knowing that it is through self-awareness that we can truly align ourselves with the divine purpose.

May Allah bless each one of you with the light of self

*Sufi Secrets to Inner Healing………...*

## Section 5.4: the Practices for Deepening Self-Knowledge and Finding Inner Healing

My dear brothers and sisters,

In this section of the Sufi secret, I will be discussing a topic that is crucial for our spiritual growth and inner healing - the practices for deepening self-knowledge and finding inner healing. In our journey towards self-discovery and self-improvement, these practices serve as transformative tools, guiding us towards a deeper understanding of ourselves and a path to inner healing.

Allah, in His infinite wisdom, reminds us in the Quran, "Indeed, Allah will not change the condition of a people until they change what is in themselves" (Quran, 13:11). This verse beautifully emphasizes the importance of self-reflection and self-improvement. It signifies that true change and healing begin from within ourselves. It is through introspection and self-awareness that we can recognize the areas that require healing and take the necessary steps to address them.

*Sufi Secrets to Inner Healing………..*

One of the most effective practices for deepening self-knowledge and finding inner healing is the act of self-reflection. Taking time out of our busy lives to introspect and reflect upon our thoughts, actions, and emotions allows us to gain insights into our inner world. The Quran encourages self-reflection, as Allah says, "Indeed, in the creation of the heavens and the earth and the alternation of the night and the day are signs for those of understanding" (Quran, 3:190). By observing the signs of Allah's creation, we can find profound lessons and contemplate the purpose of our existence.

Another practice that aids in deepening self-knowledge is seeking knowledge. Islam places great emphasis on seeking knowledge as a means of self-improvement. The Prophet Muhammad (peace be upon him) said, "Seeking knowledge is obligatory upon every Muslim." By acquiring knowledge about our religion, the world around us, and our own selves, we gain the tools necessary to navigate through life and find inner healing. The Quran affirms the importance of knowledge,

*Sufi Secrets to Inner Healing...........*

stating, "Allah will exalt in degree those of you who believe and those who have been given knowledge" (Quran, 58:11).

In addition to self-reflection and seeking knowledge, we must engage in the practice of self-care. Taking care of our physical, mental, and emotional well-being is essential for finding inner healing. The Prophet Muhammad (peace be upon him) taught us, "Your body has rights over you." This Hadith reminds us of the importance of maintaining good health and self-care. Engaging in activities such as exercise, getting enough rest, and nourishing our bodies with wholesome food contribute to our overall well-being and inner healing.

Furthermore, the practice of self-discipline plays a significant role in deepening self-knowledge and finding inner healing. By disciplining ourselves in matters of worship, time management, and controlling our desires, we gain mastery over our nafs (lower self) and develop a heightened sense of self-awareness. The Quran emphasizes self-discipline, as Allah says, "And who are guided because of their souls having disciplined them"

*Sufi Secrets to Inner Healing...........*

(Quran, 39:42). Through self-discipline, we can overcome negative habits and tendencies, paving the way for personal growth and healing.

My dear brothers and sisters,

As I continue to write to you, let us explore further practices that deepen self-knowledge and aid in finding inner healing.

Another powerful practice is engaging in self-forgiveness and seeking forgiveness from Allah. We are all prone to mistakes, shortcomings, and sins. However, harboring guilt and shame can hinder our spiritual growth and prevent us from experiencing true inner healing. The Quran reminds us, "And O my servants who have transgressed against themselves [by sinning], do not despair of the mercy of Allah. Indeed, Allah forgives all sins. Indeed, it is He who is the Forgiving, the Merciful" (Quran, 39:53). Embracing the concept of seeking forgiveness allows us to release ourselves from the burdens of our past and find solace in Allah's mercy and forgiveness.

*Sufi Secrets to Inner Healing............*

Moreover, cultivating gratitude is a transformative practice that enhances self-knowledge and promotes inner healing. Being grateful for the blessings bestowed upon us, both big and small, shifts our perspective and nurtures a positive mindset. The Quran states, "And [remember] when your Lord proclaimed, 'If you are grateful, I will surely increase you [in favor]; but if you deny, indeed, My punishment is severe'" (Quran, 14:7). Expressing gratitude to Allah not only deepens our connection with Him but also brings about a sense of contentment and inner peace.

A crucial aspect of self-knowledge and inner healing is seeking support and guidance from knowledgeable individuals. The companions of the Prophet Muhammad (peace be upon him) would seek counsel and advice from him on matters of personal and spiritual growth. Similarly, turning to trusted scholars, mentors, or counselors can provide valuable insights, guidance, and support on our journey of self-discovery and healing. It is through seeking knowledge and learning from those who have

*Sufi Secrets to Inner Healing………..*

expertise that we can navigate the challenges we face and find the healing we seek.

Finally, the practice of selfless service and helping others is a remarkable way to deepen self-knowledge and experience inner healing. The Prophet Muhammad (peace be upon him) said, "The most beloved of people to Allah are those who are most beneficial to people." Engaging in acts of kindness, charity, and serving others not only benefits those in need but also purifies our hearts and souls. It cultivates compassion, empathy, and a sense of purpose, leading to profound inner healing and fulfillment.

In my own journey as an Islamic scholar and preacher, I have witnessed the transformative power of these practices. They have allowed me to develop a deeper understanding of myself, to find healing from past wounds, and to connect with Allah on a profound level. By incorporating these practices into our lives, we can experience similar transformations and embark on a journey of self-discovery and inner healing.

*Sufi Secrets to Inner Healing...........*

My beloved brothers and sisters, let us embrace these practices with sincerity, intention, and consistency. Let us embark on a journey of self-exploration and healing, knowing that Allah is with us every step of the way. May He bless us with self-knowledge, inner healing, and a deep connection with Him. May our hearts find solace, tranquility, and fulfillment as we deepen our understanding of ourselves and draw closer to the Divine presence.

Finally, connecting with Allah through acts of worship is a fundamental practice for deepening self-knowledge and finding inner healing. Establishing a sincere and intimate relationship with our Creator allows us to find solace, guidance, and healing. The Quran states, "Verily, in the remembrance of Allah do hearts find rest" (Quran, 13:28). Engaging in acts of worship such as prayer, recitation of the Quran, and engaging in supplication (du'a) provide us with a sense of peace and tranquility.

And Allah knows best.

*Sufi Secrets to Inner Healing...........*

## Chapter Six

## Section 6.1: Surrendering to Divine Will: Finding Peace in Acceptance

My dear brothers and sisters,

Let us delve into the profound topic of surrendering to Divine Will and finding peace in acceptance. In Chapter 6 of our spiritual journey, we explore the essence of submitting to Allah's decree and embracing the path that He has destined for us.

Surrendering to Divine Will is an act of profound faith and trust in Allah's wisdom and guidance. It is recognizing that He is the All-Knowing, All-Wise, and All-Merciful. The Quran reminds us, "But perhaps you hate a thing and it is good for you; and perhaps you love a thing and it is bad for you. And Allah knows, while you know not" (Quran, 2:216). It is through this understanding that we realize that Allah's plans for us are far greater than our limited comprehension. Thus, surrendering to His Will becomes a source of peace and contentment.

*Sufi Secrets to Inner Healing...........*

In our personal lives, we may encounter situations that challenge us, disappoint us, or deviate from our expectations. However, it is in these moments that surrendering to Divine Will becomes crucial. As an Islamic scholar and preacher, I have witnessed the transformative power of embracing Allah's decree in my own life and the lives of others. There have been times when I questioned the course of events, only to realize later that it was a blessing in disguise. Allah's wisdom is infinite, and He orchestrates our lives with a purpose that surpasses our understanding.

Acceptance is a vital component of surrendering to Divine Will. It is acknowledging that Allah's plans may differ from our own desires and plans. It is recognizing that true peace lies in accepting His decree wholeheartedly. The Quran reminds us, "And it may be that you dislike a thing which is good for you and that you like a thing which is bad for you. Allah knows but you do not know" (Quran, 2:216). Acceptance allows us to align our hearts with the Divine and find solace in the knowledge that Allah is the Best of Planners.

*Sufi Secrets to Inner Healing………..*

Moreover, surrendering to Divine Will does not imply passivity or resignation in the face of challenges. It is about embracing the circumstances we find ourselves in and actively seeking the lessons and opportunities for growth within them. The Prophet Muhammad (peace be upon him) said, "How wonderful is the affair of the believer, for his affairs are all good, and this applies to no one but the believer. If something good happens to him, he is thankful for it and that is good for him. If something bad happens to him, he bears it with patience, and that is good for him" (Sahih Muslim). Surrendering to Divine Will empowers us to respond to challenges with resilience, patience, and gratitude, knowing that every experience holds a divine purpose.

In conclusion, my dear brothers and sisters, surrendering to Divine Will and finding peace in acceptance is a lifelong journey of faith, trust, and inner transformation. As an Islamic scholar and preacher, I have experienced the profound impact of surrendering to Allah's decree in my own life and witnessed its transformative power in the lives of others. May Allah bless us with the strength to surrender to His Will, to find peace in

*Sufi Secrets to Inner Healing………..*

acceptance, and to trust in His infinite wisdom. May He guide us on this spiritual journey, enveloping us in His mercy and granting us tranquility and contentment.

And Allah knows best.

*Sufi Secrets to Inner Healing…………*

## Section 6.2: The Understanding the Concept of Divine Will (Qadr)

My dear brothers and sisters,

Follow me as I go into the concept of Divine Will, also known as Qadr, and explore its significance in our lives. Understanding and embracing the concept of Divine Will is essential for us to navigate the complexities of this world with faith and conviction.

Divine Will refers to Allah's decree and His ultimate authority over all aspects of creation. It encompasses everything that occurs in the universe, from the tiniest of details to the grandest of events. Allah's Will is all-encompassing, and He has ordained every occurrence with perfect wisdom and knowledge. As the Quran states, "Indeed, We have created all things in proportion and measure" (Quran, 54:49).

As an Islamic scholar and seasoned preacher, I have witnessed the impact of understanding and accepting Divine Will in the lives of countless individuals. Embracing the concept of Divine

*Sufi Secrets to Inner Healing...........*

Will grants us peace, solace, and a deeper connection with our Creator. It allows us to surrender ourselves to the wisdom and plan of Allah, trusting that He knows what is best for us, even when we may not comprehend His decree.

One of the fundamental teachings of Islam regarding Divine Will is the concept of predestination. Allah, in His infinite knowledge and wisdom, has already ordained everything that will occur in our lives. The Quran affirms, "No disaster strikes upon the earth or among yourselves except that it is in a register before We bring it into being - indeed that, for Allah, is easy" (Quran, 57:22). This verse reminds us that nothing happens without the knowledge and permission of Allah.

Understanding Divine Will also requires us to recognize the balance between free will and destiny. Allah has granted us the ability to make choices and decisions in our lives, but ultimately, it is He who determines the outcome. We must strive to align our will with His divine plan, seeking His guidance in every aspect of our lives. The Prophet Muhammad (peace be upon

*Sufi Secrets to Inner Healing*…………

him) said, "Adhere to what is beneficial for you, seek help from Allah, and do not lose hope. And if anything befalls you, do not say, 'If only I had done such and such,' but rather say, 'Qadr Allah wa ma sha'a fa'al' (This is the decree of Allah, and what He wills, He does)" (Sahih Muslim).

Embracing the concept of Divine Will does not absolve us of personal responsibility or effort. While we acknowledge that Allah's decree is supreme, we must actively strive to fulfill our obligations, make righteous choices, and seek His guidance. We should put forth our best efforts in all aspects of our lives, knowing that the outcome ultimately rests with Allah.

In conclusion, my dear brothers and sisters, understanding and accepting the concept of Divine Will (Qadr) is a profound aspect of our faith. It requires us to have unwavering trust in Allah's wisdom and to surrender ourselves to His plan. As an Islamic scholar and preacher, I have seen the transformative power of embracing Divine Will in the lives of individuals, including my own. May Allah grant us the wisdom to comprehend His decree,

*Sufi Secrets to Inner Healing...........*

the strength to align our will with His, and the patience to accept His divine plan. May we find peace, contentment, and tranquility in submitting to His will, and may our faith in Divine Will guide us through the journey of life.

And Allah knows best.

*Sufi Secrets to Inner Healing............*

## Section 6.3: Embracing Acceptance and Letting Go

My dear brothers and sisters,

Follow me as I address you with a heart filled with gratitude and love, I invite you to embark on a profound journey of embracing acceptance and letting go. This journey is an essential aspect of our spiritual growth and a means to find solace and tranquility in the face of life's challenges.

As an Islamic scholar and seasoned preacher, I have had the privilege of witnessing the transformative power of embracing acceptance and letting go in the lives of countless individuals. It is a path that leads to inner peace and a deepening connection with Allah, our Creator.

In the Quran, Allah reminds us of the importance of acceptance, saying, "And it may be that you dislike a thing which is good for you and that you like a thing which is bad for you. Allah knows but you do not know" (Quran, 2:216). This verse teaches us that our limited human perspective may prevent us from

*Sufi Secrets to Inner Healing............*

understanding the wisdom behind certain situations. It is a call to trust in Allah's plan and surrender to His divine decree.

One of the fundamental teachings of Islam is the concept of Tawakkul, which is placing our complete trust in Allah. It is a recognition that Allah is the ultimate Planner and Controller of all affairs. The Prophet Muhammad (peace be upon him) said, "If you truly place your trust in Allah, He will provide for you as He provides for the birds. They go out in the morning hungry and return in the evening full" (Sunan Ibn Majah). This Hadith reminds us that by embracing acceptance and letting go, we open ourselves to the boundless blessings and provisions of Allah.

Embracing acceptance and letting go does not mean we become passive or indifferent to life's challenges. It means we acknowledge that there are circumstances beyond our control and we strive to respond with grace and resilience. The Prophet Muhammad (peace be upon him) beautifully demonstrated this in his own life, as he faced numerous trials and tribulations with unwavering faith and patience.

Letting go also involves releasing attachment to worldly desires and outcomes. The Quran teaches us, "But perhaps you hate a thing and it is good for you; and perhaps you love a thing and it is bad for you. And Allah knows, while you know not" (Quran, 2:216). This verse reminds us that Allah's wisdom surpasses our limited understanding, and what may appear unfavorable to us in the present moment may lead to immense blessings in the long run.

In our pursuit of embracing acceptance and letting go, we should strive to cultivate gratitude. Gratitude allows us to focus on the blessings bestowed upon us by Allah, rather than dwelling on what we perceive as lacking or unfavorable. It enables us to find contentment and joy in the present moment, even amidst difficulties.

As I conclude this sermon, my beloved brothers and sisters, I urge you to embark on the transformative journey of embracing

*Sufi Secrets to Inner Healing………..*

acceptance and letting go. Embrace the teachings of the Quran and the example of our beloved Prophet Muhammad (peace be upon him). Trust in Allah's plan, have faith in His wisdom, and surrender to His divine decree. May we find solace and inner peace in accepting what we cannot change and let go of what no longer serves us. Through acceptance and letting go, may we draw closer to Allah and experience the profound beauty of His guidance and blessings.

And Allah knows best.

## Section 6.3: Attaining Inner Peace through Surrender

My dear brothers and sisters,

I stand before you in this journey through my words with a heart filled with humility and gratitude; I invite you to explore the profound path of attaining inner peace through surrender. This path is a transformative journey that leads us closer to Allah, our Merciful Creator, and grants us the serenity and tranquility we seek in our lives.

I have witnessed firsthand the power of surrender in the lives of individuals seeking inner peace. It is a surrender that goes beyond mere resignation; rather, it is an act of profound trust and submission to the will of Allah.

In the Quran, Allah reminds us of the importance of surrendering to Him, saying, "And whoever submits his face to Allah while he is a doer of good - then he has grasped the most trustworthy handhold" (Quran, 31:22). This verse emphasizes that true inner peace comes from aligning our will with the will

*Sufi Secrets to Inner Healing...........*

of Allah and surrendering ourselves to His guidance and wisdom.

Surrendering to Allah requires us to let go of our desires for control and to acknowledge that Allah is the ultimate authority over all matters. It is a recognition that we are but servants of Allah, and our purpose in life is to worship and obey Him. The Prophet Muhammad (peace be upon him) beautifully exemplified this surrender in his own life, as he submitted to Allah's commands without hesitation and found inner peace amidst the trials and tribulations he faced.

Surrendering to Allah does not mean we become passive or resign ourselves to fate. It means we strive to align our actions and intentions with the teachings of Islam, seeking guidance from the Quran and the Sunnah of our beloved Prophet (peace be upon him). It means we trust in Allah's wisdom and accept that His plans for us are far greater than what we may envision for ourselves.

*Sufi Secrets to Inner Healing…………*

One of the most profound forms of surrender is to trust in Allah's divine timing. Allah says in the Quran, "And He will provide for him from sources he could never imagine" (Quran, 65:3). This verse reminds us that Allah's provisions and blessings are vast and encompassing. Sometimes, we may experience delays or setbacks, but through surrender, we trust that Allah's timing is perfect and that He knows what is best for us.

In our journey of attaining inner peace through surrender, we must also cultivate a state of constant remembrance of Allah. The Quran states, "Those who have believed and whose hearts are assured by the remembrance of Allah. Unquestionably, by the remembrance of Allah, hearts are assured" (Quran, 13:28). Remembering Allah in all aspects of our lives, seeking His guidance through prayer and supplication, and reciting His glorious names and attributes, all contribute to a deep sense of inner peace and tranquility.

*Sufi Secrets to Inner Healing………..*

As I conclude this sermon, my dear brothers and sisters, I urge you to embrace the path of surrender as a means to attain inner peace. Surrender to Allah with humility, trust in His divine plan, and seek His guidance in all that you do. Let go of your attachments to worldly desires and place your complete trust in the Almighty. May surrendering to Allah be the key that unlocks the door to true serenity and inner peace in your lives.

May Allah bless you all and grant you the strength and wisdom to embrace surrender and find eternal peace in His infinite mercy.

And Allah knows best.

*Sufi Secrets to Inner Healing………..*

# Chapter Seven

## Section 7.1: Arabic Wisdom: Exploring Sacred Texts and Their Healing Messages

Assalamu Alaikum wa Rahmatullahi wa Barakatuhu

My dear brothers and sisters,

I am humbled to delve into the wisdom contained within Chapter 7 of our journey, titled "Arabic Wisdom: Exploring Sacred Texts and Their Healing Messages." As an Islamic scholar, it brings me great joy to share with you the richness and depth of the Arabic language, particularly as it relates to our sacred texts—the Quran and the Hadith.

The Arabic language holds a unique place in the Islamic tradition. It is the language in which the final revelation, the Quran, was revealed to our beloved Prophet Muhammad (peace be upon him). It is a language that carries within it a powerful spiritual energy and a profound depth of meaning. Exploring the sacred texts in Arabic opens up a world of healing messages that can transform our hearts and souls.

*Sufi Secrets to Inner Healing...........*

The Quran, being the literal word of Allah, is a source of guidance and light for all humanity. It contains verses that offer solace, comfort, and healing for those who seek it. For instance, Allah says in Surah Yunus (10:57), "O mankind, there has to come to you instruction from your Lord and healing for what is in the breasts and guidance and mercy for the believers." This verse reminds us that the Quran is not only a book of guidance but also a source of healing for the ailments of the heart.

As we explore the Arabic wisdom within the sacred texts, we uncover the beauty and intricacy of the language. Each word and phrase carries immense depth and multiple layers of meaning. It is through the study and contemplation of these texts that we can discover profound healing messages tailored to our individual journeys.

The Hadith, the sayings and actions of our beloved Prophet Muhammad (peace be upon him), also provide us with guidance and wisdom. The Arabic language in which the Hadith is preserved adds to its authenticity and precision. One Hadith that

*Sufi Secrets to Inner Healing............*

highlights the importance of seeking knowledge and wisdom is when the Prophet (peace be upon him) said, "Whoever follows a path in the pursuit of knowledge, Allah will make a path to Paradise easy for him" (Sahih Muslim).

Exploring the sacred texts in Arabic allows us to connect with the essence of the messages conveyed. It enables us to uncover the subtleties, nuances, and spiritual insights embedded within the verses. It is a journey of deep reflection, contemplation, and internalization. When we recite the Quran in Arabic, even if we may not fully grasp the language's intricacies, we open our hearts to receive the healing energy and divine wisdom contained within the words.

As an Islamic scholar and seasoned preacher, I have personally experienced the transformative power of delving into the Arabic wisdom of the sacred texts. It is a journey that not only deepens our understanding but also nourishes our souls and brings us closer to Allah. It is through this exploration that we find solace

*Sufi Secrets to Inner Healing…………*

in times of distress, guidance in times of confusion, and healing in times of pain.

I encourage each one of you to embark on this journey of exploring the sacred texts in their original Arabic form. Whether it is through studying the Quran, reflecting on its meanings, or seeking guidance from the Hadith, immerse yourself in the language of revelation. Let the healing messages within these texts resonate within your hearts and illuminate your path.

May Allah bless us all with the ability to delve into the Arabic wisdom of our sacred texts. May our exploration bring us closer to Allah, grant us healing and tranquility, and guide us on the straight path. And may our hearts be filled with gratitude for the blessing of the Quran and the Hadith.

And Allah knows best.

*Sufi Secrets to Inner Healing………..*

## Section 7.2: The Quranic Verses of Healing and Solace

My respected brothers and sisters,

In this section, I will be exploring the profound healing and solace that the Quran offers. As an Islamic scholar and seasoned preacher, I have witnessed the transformative power of the Quranic verses in the lives of countless individuals. It is through the Quran that we find guidance, comfort, and healing for our physical, emotional, and spiritual well-being.

The Quran, the final revelation from Allah, is a divine gift to humanity. It contains verses that speak directly to our hearts, offering solace in times of distress and healing for our souls. Allah, in His infinite wisdom and mercy, has provided us with a guidebook for life, encompassing every aspect of our existence.

In Surah Al-Isra (17:82), Allah assures us, "And We send down of the Qur'an that which is healing and mercy for the believers." This verse reminds us that the Quran is not merely a collection of words, but a divine prescription for healing and a source of mercy from our Creator.

*Sufi Secrets to Inner Healing...........*

Throughout the Quran, we find verses that address our physical ailments, emotional burdens, and spiritual struggles. Allah, out of His infinite compassion, has provided us with the means to seek solace and healing through His words.

One of the most well-known verses of healing is found in Surah Al-Fatiha (1:6-7), where we recite, "Guide us to the straight path - the path of those upon whom You have bestowed favor, not of those who have evoked anger or of those who are astray." This verse serves as a powerful reminder that seeking Allah's guidance and staying on the straight path is the ultimate source of healing and solace.

In Surah Al-Sharh (94:5-6), Allah says, "Indeed, with hardship, there is ease. Indeed, with hardship, there is ease." These verses offer comfort and assurance during times of difficulty, reminding us that for every hardship we face, there is relief and ease that follows.

The Quran also addresses matters of the heart and emotional well-being. In Surah Ar-Rad (13:28), Allah says, "Those who

*Sufi Secrets to Inner Healing*………..

have believed and whose hearts are assured by the remembrance of Allah. Unquestionably, by the remembrance of Allah, hearts are assured." This verse emphasizes the importance of remembering Allah and seeking solace in His remembrance, for it brings tranquility and peace to our hearts.

Furthermore, the Quran guides us on the path to spiritual healing. In Surah Al-Hijr (15:97), Allah states, "Indeed, We have sent down to you a Book [i.e., the Qur'an] in which is your mention. Then will you not reason?" This verse invites us to reflect upon the words of the Quran, for it is in reflection and contemplation that we find spiritual enlightenment and healing.

As an Islamic scholar and seasoned preacher, I have personally witnessed the transformative impact of the Quranic verses of healing and solace. I have seen individuals find peace in times of distress, comfort in times of grief, and strength in times of weakness, all through the guidance of the Quran.

I encourage each one of you to establish a deep connection with the Quran. Take time to recite its verses, reflect upon their

*Sufi Secrets to Inner Healing...........*

meanings, and internalize their teachings. Seek solace in the divine words and let them guide you on your journey of healing and spiritual growth.

Let us not forget the words of our beloved Prophet Muhammad (peace be upon him) who said, "The best of you are those who learn the Quran and teach it." Let us strive to be among those who not only seek healing through the Quran but also share its wisdom and healing messages with others.

May Allah bless us all with the ability to immerse ourselves in the divine teachings.

*Sufi Secrets to Inner Healing…………*

## Section 7.3: Hadiths on Emotional and Spiritual Well-being

Assalamualaikum, my dear brothers and sisters,

Welcome to this enlightening section where I will illuminate the significance of emotional and spiritual well-being in light of the Hadiths of our beloved Prophet Muhammad (peace be upon him).. As an Islamic scholar and seasoned preacher, I have had the privilege of studying and reflecting upon the profound wisdom contained in the Hadiths, which offer guidance for every aspect of our lives.

The teachings of Prophet Muhammad (peace be upon him) encompass not only matters of worship and daily conduct but also provide invaluable insights into nurturing our emotional and spiritual well-being. His words serve as a source of inspiration, solace, and guidance, reminding us of the path towards attaining tranquility and contentment in this world and the Hereafter.

One of the Hadiths that emphasizes the significance of emotional well-being is when the Prophet (peace be upon him)

*Sufi Secrets to Inner Healing………..*

said, "None of you truly believes until he loves for his brother what he loves for himself" (Sahih Bukhari, Book 1, Hadith 13). This Hadith reminds us of the importance of cultivating love and empathy towards others. By embracing this teaching, we create an environment of emotional support, compassion, and unity within our communities.

In another Hadith, the Prophet (peace be upon him) beautifully illustrates the connection between the heart and spiritual well-being. He said, "Indeed, in the body, there is a piece of flesh, which if it is sound, the whole body will be sound, and if it is corrupt, the whole body will be corrupt. Verily, it is the heart" (Sahih Bukhari, Book 1, Hadith 49). This profound Hadith emphasizes the centrality of a pure and healthy heart in achieving spiritual well-being. It highlights the need to purify our intentions, cultivate sincere faith, and guard against spiritual diseases such as envy, arrogance, and greed.

The Prophet Muhammad (peace be upon him) also provided guidance on maintaining emotional balance and seeking solace

*Sufi Secrets to Inner Healing............*

in challenging times. He said, "Know that victory comes with patience, relief with affliction, and ease with hardship" (Sunan Ibn Majah, Book 37, Hadith 4296). This Hadith reminds us that difficulties are part of our journey, but with patience and trust in Allah, we can find relief and ultimately achieve victory. It serves as a source of comfort, assuring us that our struggles are not in vain and that they are a means for our growth and spiritual elevation.

Furthermore, the Prophet (peace be upon him) emphasized the importance of seeking knowledge for our emotional and spiritual well-being. He said, "Seeking knowledge is obligatory upon every Muslim" (Sunan Ibn Majah, Book 1, Hadith 224). By seeking knowledge of Islam, understanding the Quran, and studying the Hadiths, we equip ourselves with the tools necessary to navigate the challenges of life and cultivate a strong connection with Allah.

As an Islamic scholar and seasoned preacher, I have personally witnessed the transformative power of these Hadiths in the lives

*Sufi Secrets to Inner Healing………..*

of individuals. The wisdom contained within them offers profound insights into nurturing our emotional well-being, fostering healthy relationships, and attaining spiritual growth.

Let us strive to implement the teachings of our beloved Prophet Muhammad (peace be upon him) in our lives. Let us cultivate love, empathy, and compassion towards one another, purify our hearts, and seek knowledge that strengthens our faith and nurtures our emotional and spiritual well-being.

May Allah bless us all with emotional and spiritual well-being, and may He grant us the ability to follow the footsteps of our beloved Prophet Muhammad (peace be upon him). Ameen.

And Allah knows best.

*Sufi Secrets to Inner Healing………..*

## Section 7.4: the Beauty and Depth of Arabic Calligraphy

Bismillah ar-Rahman ar-Rahim. Assalamu Alaikum wa Rahmatullahi wa Barakatuhu.

Dear brothers and sisters in faith, in this section I want to reflect upon the beauty and depth of Arabic calligraphy, a remarkable art form that has captivated hearts and minds for centuries. As an Islamic scholar and a lover of the Quran, I am deeply inspired by the intricate strokes and mesmerizing patterns that adorn the pages of our sacred scripture. Allow me to share with you the significance and spiritual dimensions of Arabic calligraphy.

Arabic calligraphy holds a special place in Islamic culture and tradition. It is not merely an art form, but a means of connecting with the divine. The written word carries immense power, and when combined with the artistry of calligraphy, it becomes a visual representation of the sacred. Each stroke and curve holds meaning and intention, reflecting the beauty and wisdom of the words it portrays.

*Sufi Secrets to Inner Healing………..*

In the Quran, Allah says in Surah Al-Qalam (68:4): "And indeed, you are of a great moral character." This verse not only speaks to the noble character of the Prophet Muhammad (peace be upon him) but also highlights the importance of aesthetics and beauty in our lives. Arabic calligraphy allows us to manifest this beauty through written words, turning them into artistic expressions that transcend the mundane and elevate our souls.

The Prophet Muhammad (peace be upon him) once said, "Allah is beautiful and loves beauty." This profound statement reminds us that our Creator appreciates and values beauty in all its forms. Arabic calligraphy is a testament to this truth, as it embodies the pursuit of excellence and perfection in artistic expression. When we witness the delicate strokes and intricate designs, we are reminded of the beauty and magnificence of Allah's creation.

Moreover, Arabic calligraphy serves as a powerful tool for conveying the messages of the Quran and Hadith. It enhances our understanding and appreciation of the sacred texts by visually emphasizing the words and themes they contain. As we

*Sufi Secrets to Inner Healing...........*

engage with the calligraphic art, we immerse ourselves in the teachings of Islam and draw closer to Allah.

When I contemplate Arabic calligraphy, I am reminded of the verse in Surah Al-Isra (17:82) where Allah says, "And We send down of the Quran that which is healing and mercy for the believers." The beauty of Arabic calligraphy not only captivates our eyes but also soothes our hearts and nourishes our souls. It is a visual representation of the healing and mercy embedded within the words of the Quran.

In conclusion, Arabic calligraphy is a profound expression of faith, beauty, and divine revelation. Through its intricate designs and skilled craftsmanship, it enhances our connection with the Quran and Hadith, and it elevates our spiritual journey. Let us embrace and celebrate the art of Arabic calligraphy, recognizing it as a gift from Allah that enriches our lives and strengthens our faith.

*Sufi Secrets to Inner Healing………..*

May Allah bless us with a deep appreciation for the beauty of Arabic calligraphy and guide us to embody the wisdom and spirituality it represents. Ameen.

Wa Allahu 'Alam.

## Chapter Eight

### Section 8.1: The Sufi Path to Compassion and Service

Bismillah ar-Rahman ar-Rahim. Assalamu Alaikum wa Rahmatullahi wa Barakatuhu.

Dear brothers and sisters in faith, I invite you to stay connected as I delve into the profound teachings of Chapter 8: The Sufi Path to Compassion and Service. As an Islamic scholar and a seeker on the spiritual path, I am deeply inspired by the wisdom and transformative power of Sufism. Let us embark on this spiritual journey together and explore the path of compassion and service.

Sufism, often referred to as the mystical dimension of Islam, holds a special place in our tradition. It encompasses the pursuit of a deeper understanding of the Divine and the realization of our true selves in relation to Allah. Sufis strive to cultivate a heart filled with love, compassion, and empathy, and they channel these virtues into acts of service and devotion to others.

*Sufi Secrets to Inner Healing………..*

Allah reminds us in the Quran in Surah Al-Baqarah (2:195): "And spend in the way of Allah and do not throw [yourselves] with your [own] hands into destruction [by refraining]." This verse encapsulates the essence of the Sufi path, as it emphasizes the importance of selfless giving and serving the needs of others. True compassion and service come from a sincere desire to please Allah and benefit His creation.

The Prophet Muhammad (peace be upon him) serves as the ultimate role model for us in embodying compassion and selfless service. He said, "The best among you are those who are best to their families, and I am the best to my family." This hadith highlights the significance of compassion and service within our own families. It reminds us that true spirituality is not confined to rituals and acts of worship alone, but it extends to our relationships and interactions with those closest to us.

Sufism teaches us that the path to compassion and service begins with self-awareness and self-purification. As we strive to cultivate a heart that is free from ego-driven desires and

*Sufi Secrets to Inner Healing………..*

attachments, we become more receptive to the needs and suffering of others. The purification of the self allows us to empathize with the pain and struggles of our fellow human beings, and it fuels our determination to alleviate their suffering.

In Surah Al-Hujurat (49:10), Allah says, "The believers are but brothers, so make settlement between your brothers. And fear Allah that you may receive mercy." This verse emphasizes the importance of unity, cooperation, and compassion among believers. It calls us to be agents of peace and reconciliation, not only within our own community but also in society at large. It is through acts of kindness, forgiveness, and understanding that we manifest the true essence of Islam.

Sufism teaches us to go beyond the superficial differences that divide us and to recognize the inherent humanity in every individual. We are encouraged to extend compassion and service to all, regardless of their social status, ethnicity, or faith. The Prophet Muhammad (peace be upon him) said, "He who has no compassion for others will not receive compassion." This hadith

*Sufi Secrets to Inner Healing………..*

reminds us that our compassion and service should extend beyond our comfort zones, reaching those who are marginalized and in need.

As I reflect on my own journey, I am reminded of the profound impact that practicing compassion and engaging in acts of service has had on my own spiritual growth. It is through these actions that I have witnessed the transformative power of love and the beauty of selfless giving.

In the pursuit of compassion and service, we must remember that it is not just about external acts but also about the intention and sincerity behind our actions. Our Prophet Muhammad (peace be upon him) said, "Actions are judged by intentions, and everyone will be rewarded according to what they intended." This hadith teaches us that our intentions should be pure and solely for the sake of pleasing Allah and seeking His pleasure.

Sufi teachings remind us that true compassion arises from recognizing the inherent unity of all creation. It is an expression of our interconnectedness and our responsibility to care for one

*Sufi Secrets to Inner Healing………..*

another. Allah says in the Quran in Surah Al-Ma'idah (5:32), "And whoever saves one [a life], it is as if he had saved mankind entirely." This verse emphasizes the value and sanctity of every human life and encourages us to extend our compassion and service to all.

Furthermore, Sufism emphasizes the practice of selflessness and humility. It teaches us to let go of our ego, our attachment to material possessions, and our desire for recognition. The Prophet Muhammad (peace be upon him) said, "The best of people are those who bring most benefit to others." This hadith reminds us that our service should not be driven by personal gain or recognition but rather by a genuine desire to benefit others and seek the pleasure of Allah.

In our pursuit of compassion and service, we may face challenges and obstacles. It is important to remain steadfast in our commitment, knowing that our efforts are ultimately for the sake of Allah. Allah assures us in the Quran in Surah Al-Inshirah (94:5-6), "Verily, with hardship, there is relief. Verily,

*Sufi Secrets to Inner Healing………..*

with hardship, there is relief." These verses remind us that even in times of difficulty, there is always comfort and ease that follows. So, let us persevere and remain steadfast in our journey of compassion and service.

Dear brothers and sisters, as we reflect upon the teachings of Sufism and the path to compassion and service, let us remember that true transformation occurs when we internalize these values and allow them to shape our thoughts, actions, and interactions with others. May our hearts be filled with love, empathy, and a genuine desire to alleviate the suffering of others.

Let us be inspired by the examples of the great Sufi saints and scholars who dedicated their lives to service, and strive to follow in their footsteps. By embodying compassion and selfless service, we not only bring solace to those in need but also purify our own souls and draw closer to the Divine.

In conclusion, the Sufi path to compassion and service is a profound and transformative journey. It calls us to embrace the teachings of the Quran and the example of the Prophet

*Sufi Secrets to Inner Healing…………*

Muhammad (peace be upon him), and to embody love, empathy, and selflessness in all aspects of our lives. May Allah bless us with the strength, wisdom, and guidance to walk this path with sincerity and devotion.

May we become beacons of compassion and service, spreading love and light in a world that is in desperate need of healing. May our actions inspire others and draw them closer to the path of Islam. And may our commitment to compassion and service be a means of attaining the pleasure of Allah and the ultimate reward of Paradise.

Assalamu Alaikum wa Rahmatullahi wa Barakatuhu.

*Sufi Secrets to Inner Healing………..*

## Section 8.2: Compassion as a Transformative Force

Bismillahir Rahmanir Rahim.

All praise and thanks are due to Allah, the Most Merciful, the Compassionate. May His peace and blessings be upon our beloved Prophet Muhammad (peace be upon him), his family, and his companions.

Dear brothers and sisters in Islam, today I want to speak to you about the transformative power of compassion. As an Islamic scholar and seasoned preacher, I have witnessed firsthand the profound impact that compassion can have on individuals, communities, and the world at large.

Compassion is a fundamental value in Islam, rooted in the teachings of the Quran and the noble example of our Prophet Muhammad (peace be upon him). Allah, the Most Compassionate, describes Himself in Surah Al-An'am (6:12), saying, "And to Allah belongs the best names, so invoke Him by them. And leave [the company of] those who practice deviation concerning His names. They will be recompensed for what they

*Sufi Secrets to Inner Healing...........*

have been doing." This verse highlights Allah's attribute of compassion and encourages us to invoke Him by His beautiful names, including the Most Compassionate.

The Prophet Muhammad (peace be upon him) exemplified compassion in his interactions with people. He said, "The merciful ones are granted mercy by the Most Merciful. Be merciful to those on the earth, and the One above the heavens will have mercy upon you." This hadith emphasizes the reciprocal nature of compassion, indicating that when we show mercy and compassion to others, Allah, the Most Merciful, showers His mercy upon us.

Compassion is not limited to acts of kindness and generosity; it extends to our words, thoughts, and intentions. The Prophet Muhammad (peace be upon him) said, "Do not belittle any act of kindness, even if it is greeting your brother with a cheerful face." This hadith reminds us that even a small act of compassion, such as a smile or a kind word, holds immense value in the sight of Allah.

*Sufi Secrets to Inner Healing………..*

Furthermore, the Quran teaches us that compassion is not reserved solely for our fellow Muslims but extends to all of humanity. In Surah Al-Hujurat (49:13), Allah says, "O mankind, indeed We have created you from male and female and made you peoples and tribes that you may know one another. Indeed, the most noble of you in the sight of Allah is the most righteous of you." This verse highlights the importance of recognizing the inherent worth and dignity of every human being, regardless of their background or beliefs.

As we strive to cultivate compassion in our lives, we must remember that it requires empathy and understanding. We must seek to alleviate the suffering of others and work towards creating a more just and compassionate society. The Prophet Muhammad (peace be upon him) said, "None of you truly believes until he loves for his brother what he loves for himself." This hadith underscores the importance of empathy, as it encourages us to extend the same care and concern to others that we would want for ourselves.

*Sufi Secrets to Inner Healing...........*

Compassion has the power to transform individuals and societies. It creates an atmosphere of love, unity, and understanding. When we approach others with compassion, we foster a sense of belonging and acceptance. We uplift those who are downtrodden, offer solace to the grieving, and lend a helping hand to those in need.

In our fast-paced and often self-centered world, compassion is a healing balm that brings people together and nurtures the human spirit. It breaks down barriers, promotes harmony, and fosters a sense of shared humanity.

Dear brothers and sisters, let us strive to be ambassadors of compassion in our daily lives. Let us embody the teachings of the Quran and the example of the Prophet Muhammad (peace be upon him) by showing kindness, empathy, and mercy to all those around us. Let us remember the words of Allah in Surah Al-Balad (90:17-18), "And what can make you know what is [breaking through] the difficult pass? It is the freeing of a slave or feeding on a day of severe hunger." These verses remind us of

*Sufi Secrets to Inner Healing...........*

the immense reward and significance of acts of compassion and charity.

Compassion is not limited to grand gestures; it can be expressed in the smallest of actions. It can be offering a helping hand to someone in need, listening attentively to someone's troubles, or offering a comforting word to someone who is going through a difficult time. It can also mean advocating for justice and speaking up against injustice.

As we strive to embody compassion, we must also remember that it starts from within. We must cultivate self-compassion and treat ourselves with kindness and understanding. The Prophet Muhammad (peace be upon him) said, "None of you truly believes until he loves for his brother what he loves for himself." This hadith reminds us that compassion begins with self-love and extends to others.

Dear brothers and sisters, let us make a conscious effort to cultivate compassion in our hearts and actions. Let us seek opportunities to serve others, to uplift the downtrodden, and to

*Sufi Secrets to Inner Healing……….*

spread kindness wherever we go. By doing so, we not only benefit those around us but also purify our own souls and draw closer to Allah's mercy.

In conclusion, the beauty and depth of compassion in Islam are evident in the teachings of the Quran and the example of the Prophet Muhammad (peace be upon him). It is a transformative force that has the power to heal hearts, bridge divides, and bring about positive change in the world. May Allah bless us all with hearts filled with compassion and guide us to be beacons of mercy and love in our communities. Ameen.

And Allah knows best.

*Sufi Secrets to Inner Healing…………*

## Section 8.3: The Relationship between Selflessness and Inner Healing

Bismillah Ar-Rahman Ar-Rahim.

All praise is due to Allah, the Most Merciful, the Compassionate. May His peace and blessings be upon our beloved Prophet Muhammad, his family, and his companions.

Dear brothers and sisters in Islam, As-Salamu Alaikum.

I will be reflecting upon the profound relationship between selflessness and inner healing. As believers, we are called upon to cultivate a selfless mindset and strive towards selflessness in our thoughts, actions, and interactions with others. The Quran and the teachings of our Prophet Muhammad (peace be upon him) provide us with guidance and wisdom on this transformative aspect of our spiritual journey.

Selflessness, or "ithar" in Arabic, is the act of placing the needs and interests of others above our own. It is an expression of genuine care and concern for the well-being of our fellow human beings, driven by a deep sense of compassion and

*Sufi Secrets to Inner Healing...........*

empathy. In Surah Al-Hashr (59:9), Allah says, "They give preference over themselves, even though they are in need." This verse highlights the virtue of selflessness and reminds us of the exemplary behavior of the early Muslims.

In the life of our beloved Prophet Muhammad (peace be upon him), we find numerous examples of selflessness. His entire life was a testament to putting the needs of others before his own. He would prioritize the well-being of his companions and the community, even when faced with personal challenges. His selfless actions and noble character continue to inspire us to this day.

Selflessness has a profound impact on our inner healing and spiritual growth. When we practice selflessness, we detach ourselves from the ego-driven desires and self-centeredness that often cause inner turmoil and discontentment. By shifting our focus to serving and benefiting others, we find solace and contentment in the pleasure of Allah.

*Sufi Secrets to Inner Healing………..*

Furthermore, selflessness allows us to establish meaningful connections and foster a sense of unity within the ummah. When we selflessly lend a helping hand to our brothers and sisters in need, we strengthen the bonds of brotherhood and sisterhood. This sense of unity and collective responsibility not only brings us closer to Allah but also contributes to our own inner healing and well-being.

Dear brothers and sisters, I would like to share a personal experience as an Islamic scholar and seasoned preacher. In my interactions with individuals and communities, I have witnessed the transformative power of selflessness. I have seen how acts of kindness, generosity, and self-sacrifice can heal wounded hearts, mend broken relationships, and bring profound joy and fulfillment.

When we selflessly give of ourselves, whether it is our time, resources, or expertise, we experience a sense of purpose and fulfillment that cannot be achieved through self-centered pursuits. Our hearts become purified, and we find inner peace

*Sufi Secrets to Inner Healing………..*

and tranquility in knowing that we have made a positive difference in someone's life.

In a hadith narrated by Imam Bukhari, the Prophet Muhammad (peace be upon him) said, "The one who relieves a believer's distress of the distressful aspects of this world, Allah will relieve him of a distress of the distressful aspects of the Day of Resurrection."

Brothers and sisters, let us strive to cultivate selflessness in our lives. Let us seek opportunities to serve others, uplift the oppressed, and bring joy to those who are suffering. Let us remember that selflessness is not limited to grand gestures; even small acts of kindness and compassion can have a profound impact.

As we reflect on the beauty and depth of selflessness, let us remember that our ultimate role model is our beloved Prophet Muhammad (peace be upon him). His selfless character serves as a shining example for us to emulate in our daily lives.

*Sufi Secrets to Inner Healing...........*

In Surah Al-Imran (3:31), Allah says, "Say, [O Muhammad], 'If you should love Allah, then follow me, [so] Allah will love you and forgive you your sins. And Allah is Forgiving and Merciful.'" By following the footsteps of the Prophet Muhammad (peace be upon him) and embodying his selfless nature, we draw closer to Allah's love and mercy.

Dear brothers and sisters, as we strive to deepen our understanding of selflessness and its role in our spiritual journey, let us remember that selflessness is not just a temporary act but a way of life. It requires consistent effort, self-reflection, and a genuine intention to seek the pleasure of Allah.

Let us make a commitment today to prioritize selflessness in all aspects of our lives. Let us be mindful of the needs of those around us and seize every opportunity to extend a helping hand. Whether it is through acts of charity, volunteering, or offering emotional support, let us strive to make a positive difference in the lives of others.

*Sufi Secrets to Inner Healing……….*

In doing so, we will not only experience inner healing and tranquility but also contribute to building a more compassionate and harmonious society. The world is in need of individuals who embody the spirit of selflessness and serve as beacons of light and hope.

In conclusion, the relationship between selflessness and inner healing is undeniable. By practicing selflessness, we not only heal our own hearts but also contribute to the healing of our communities and the world at large.

May Allah grant us the strength and guidance to embody selflessness, and may our actions be driven by sincere intentions, rooted in love for the sake of Allah alone.

I pray that Allah instills within us the true understanding of selflessness and enables us to be a source of comfort and support for others. May our journey towards selflessness be a means of attaining closeness to Allah and finding true fulfillment in this world and the Hereafter.

Wa-Salaamu Alaikum warahmatullahi wabarakatuh.

*Sufi Secrets to Inner Healing………..*

## Section 8.4: Engaging in Acts of Service and Kindness

Assalamu Alaikum warahmatullahi wabarakatuh,

Dear brothers and sisters,

In this section, I want to emphasize the significance of engaging in acts of service and kindness as an integral part of our Islamic faith. As Muslims, we are called upon to follow the example of our beloved Prophet Muhammad (peace be upon him) and embody the spirit of compassion and generosity in our interactions with others.

Allah, in His infinite wisdom, says in the Quran (Surah Al-Baqarah, 2:177), "Righteousness is not that you turn your faces toward the east or the west, but [true] righteousness is [in] one who believes in Allah, the Last Day, the angels, the Book, and the prophets and gives wealth, in spite of love for it, to relatives, orphans, the needy, the traveler, those who ask [for help], and for freeing slaves; [and who] establishes prayer and gives zakah; [those who] fulfill their promise when they promise; and [those who] are patient in poverty and hardship and during battle.

*Sufi Secrets to Inner Healing*............

Those are the ones who have been true, and it is those who are the righteous."

From this verse, we learn that righteousness is not limited to ritualistic acts of worship, but it encompasses our actions towards others, especially those who are in need. Engaging in acts of service and kindness is a means of expressing our faith and demonstrating our love for Allah and His creation.

The Prophet Muhammad (peace be upon him) said in a hadith recorded by Imam Muslim, "The best among you are those who benefit others." This profound statement emphasizes the importance of selflessness and the virtue of serving others. When we engage in acts of service, we are not only benefiting those in need but also purifying our hearts and drawing closer to Allah.

Dear brothers and sisters, acts of service and kindness can take various forms. It can be as simple as a smile, a kind word, or a helping hand. It can be offering assistance to a neighbor, volunteering in charitable organizations, or supporting those facing hardships in our community. Whatever form it takes, the intention behind our actions should always be sincere, seeking the pleasure of Allah.

Allah reminds us in the Quran (Surah Al-Hadid, 57:11), "Who is it that would loan Allah a goodly loan so He may multiply it for him many times over? And it is Allah who withholds and grants abundance, and to Him you will be returned." When we engage in acts of service, we are essentially lending to Allah, and He promises to multiply our rewards manifold in this world and the Hereafter.

I personally have witnessed the transformative power of acts of service in my own life. Through my years as an Islamic scholar and preacher, I have had the opportunity to engage in various charitable initiatives and witness firsthand the impact it has on individuals and communities. Not only does it bring joy and relief to those in need, but it also fills our hearts with a sense of fulfillment and contentment.

*Sufi Secrets to Inner Healing............*

Dear brothers and sisters, let us make a conscious effort to incorporate acts of service and kindness into our daily lives. Let us seek out opportunities to serve others, to uplift the downtrodden, and to spread compassion and mercy in our interactions.

As we continue our discussion on engaging in acts of service and kindness, let us reflect on the profound impact these actions can have on our own spiritual growth and well-being.

When we engage in acts of service, we align ourselves with the divine attributes of mercy, compassion, and generosity. Allah, in His infinite wisdom, has created us as social beings, and through acts of service, we strengthen the bonds of brotherhood and sisterhood within our community.

In the Quran, Allah says (Surah Al-Ma'idah, 5:2), "And cooperate in righteousness and piety, but do not cooperate in sin and aggression." This verse highlights the importance of collaborating with one another in acts of righteousness. When

*Sufi Secrets to Inner Healing............*

we join hands to serve those in need, we create a collective impact that far surpasses what we could achieve individually.

Moreover, acts of service and kindness remind us of the transient nature of this world and the blessings bestowed upon us by Allah. When we witness the struggles and hardships faced by others, it humbles us and reminds us to be grateful for the blessings we often take for granted. It is through acts of service that we develop empathy and compassion, allowing us to become more mindful of the needs of others.

The Prophet Muhammad (peace be upon him) said in a hadith recorded by Imam Bukhari, "The best of people are those who are most beneficial to people." By engaging in acts of service, we become instruments of goodness and blessings in the lives of others. Whether it is providing food to the hungry, clothing to the needy, or offering emotional support to those in distress, each act of kindness has the potential to uplift and transform lives.

*Sufi Secrets to Inner Healing…………*

Furthermore, acts of service are not limited to material assistance alone. We can also serve others through our knowledge, skills, and talents. Teaching, mentoring, and sharing our expertise with others are all valuable forms of service. Through these actions, we contribute to the intellectual and spiritual development of our community.

I personally have experienced the immense joy and fulfillment that comes from engaging in acts of service. Whether it was participating in humanitarian missions, organizing community outreach programs, or providing educational support, each experience has left a lasting impact on my own spiritual growth and development. It is through serving others that I have witnessed the profound transformation that occurs when we put the needs of others before our own.

Dear brothers and sisters, let us strive to make acts of service and kindness a consistent part of our lives. Let us remember that even the smallest acts of kindness have the potential to make a significant difference in the lives of others. Whether it is a smile,

*Sufi Secrets to Inner Healing...........*

a kind word, or a gesture of assistance, let us seize every opportunity to spread love, compassion, and mercy.

In conclusion, acts of service and kindness are not only a means of benefitting others but also a path towards self-improvement and spiritual elevation. By engaging in these noble actions, we embody the true essence of our Islamic faith and draw closer to Allah. May Allah bless us with the ability and sincerity to serve others, and may He accept our efforts and reward us abundantly.

Assalamu Alaikum warahmatullahi wabarakatuh.

*Sufi Secrets to Inner Healing…………*

# Chapter Nine

## Section 9.1: The Dance of Whirling: A Sacred Expression of Healing and Unity

Bismillahir Rahmanir Rahim (In the name of Allah, the Most Gracious, the Most Merciful)

Dear brothers and sisters,

I stand before you with my words to share the profound and sacred practice of whirling, a dance that holds deep spiritual significance within the Islamic tradition. This dance, known as Sufi whirling or sema, is not only a mesmerizing form of artistic expression but also a profound path to healing and unity.

The practice of whirling finds its roots in the teachings of the great Persian poet and mystic, Jalaluddin Rumi. Rumi, whose poetry continues to inspire hearts and minds to this day, used the metaphor of whirling to symbolize the soul's journey towards union with the Divine. He wrote, "Dance, when you're broken open. Dance, if you've torn the bandage off. Dance in the middle

*Sufi Secrets to Inner Healing...........*

of the fighting. Dance in your blood. Dance when you're perfectly free."

In the Quran, Allah calls us to reflect upon the wonders of His creation. He says (Surah Al-Jathiyah, 45:13), "And [He has subjected] to you whatever is in the heavens and whatever is on the earth - all from Him. Indeed, in that are signs for a people who give thought." Whirling, with its graceful movements and meditative rhythm, allows us to connect with the beauty and harmony of Allah's creation. It is a reminder of our place in the cosmic order and the unity of all creation.

Furthermore, the act of whirling holds deep symbolism. As the Sufis spin in circles, they symbolize the rotation of the planets, the movement of the celestial bodies, and the cycles of life and death. Through this physical manifestation, the whirling dance becomes a spiritual journey, a seeking of inner harmony and alignment with the divine will.

In the Hadith, the Prophet Muhammad (peace be upon him) said, "My Lord taught me excellent manners and then said to me,

*Sufi Secrets to Inner Healing………..*

'There is none among My servants who draws closer to Me with anything more loved by Me than the religious duties I have enjoined upon him. My servant continues to draw near to Me with supererogatory works so that I shall love him. When I love him, I am his hearing with which he hears, his seeing with which he sees, his hand with which he strikes, and his leg with which he walks. Were he to ask [something] of Me, I would surely give it to him, and were he to ask Me for refuge, I would surely grant him it'" (Recorded in Al-Bukhari).

Through the whirling dance, Sufis embark on a transformative journey of self-discovery and surrender to the divine will. The spinning motion represents the shedding of worldly attachments and ego, allowing the seeker to transcend the confines of the material world and experience a state of spiritual ecstasy and union with Allah.

I have had the privilege of witnessing the power and beauty of the whirling dance firsthand. As I observed the dervishes gracefully spin in their vibrant garments, I was reminded of the eternal quest for inner purification and spiritual elevation. The rhythmic movements and the focused attention on the divine remembrance filled the atmosphere with a sense of tranquility and awe.

Dear brothers and sisters, the whirling dance is not limited to a select few. It is a practice that invites every seeker, regardless of age, gender, or background, to embark on their own spiritual journey. It is a reminder that the path to Allah is open to all who seek Him with sincerity and devotion.

As we reflect on the significance of the whirling dance, let us remember that it is not merely a physical act but a profound spiritual practice.

May we strive to incorporate the essence of the whirling dance into our own lives, even if we may not physically spin in circles. Let us embrace the teachings it imparts and embody its symbolism in our daily actions.

First and foremost, the whirling dance teaches us the importance of remembrance and mindfulness of Allah. Just as the dervishes enter a state of focused concentration during their spins, we too should strive to be fully present in our worship, prayers, and daily activities. Let us remember the words of Allah in the Quran (Surah Al-Dhariyat, 51:56), "And I did not create the jinn and mankind except to worship Me."

Furthermore, the whirling dance emphasizes the concept of surrender and letting go. As the dervishes spin, they surrender their control and trust in the divine will. This reminds us to relinquish our attachment to worldly desires and submit to the plans and decrees of Allah. We are reminded of the words of Prophet Muhammad (peace be upon him) who said, "The strong believer is better and more beloved to Allah than the weak believer, although there is good in both. Strive for that which will benefit you, seek help from Allah, and do not despair. If a mishap should happen to befall you, then do not say, 'If only I had acted differently, it would have been such-and-such.' Rather say, 'Qadr Allah wa ma sha'a fa'al' (This is from the Decree of Allah, and He does whatever He wills)" (Recorded in Muslim).

*Sufi Secrets to Inner Healing............*

In addition to surrender, the whirling dance teaches us the importance of unity and interconnectedness. As the dervishes spin in unison, they symbolize the harmony and unity of creation. This serves as a reminder that we are all connected as part of the broader human family. Our actions, both big and small, can have a profound impact on others. Let us strive to foster unity and compassion in our interactions, seeking to alleviate the suffering of others and spread kindness and love.

The whirling dance is also a call to self-transcendence. As the dervishes whirl, they move beyond their individual selves and merge into the divine presence. This signifies the importance of rising above our ego, selfish desires, and material attachments. By doing so, we open ourselves to the transformative power of Allah's love and mercy. Allah reminds us in the Quran (Surah Al-Hujurat, 49:13), "O mankind, indeed We have created you from male and female and made you peoples and tribes that you may know one another. Indeed, the most noble of you in the sight of Allah is the most righteous of you."

*Sufi Secrets to Inner Healing...........*

Dear brothers and sisters, as we contemplate the significance of the whirling dance, let us seek to embody its teachings in our lives. May we remember to be mindful of Allah, surrender to His will, foster unity and compassion, and transcend our egos. Just as the whirling dance is a sacred expression of healing and unity, let our lives be a testament to the beauty and depth of our faith.

In conclusion, let us strive to walk the Sufi path of compassion and service, drawing inspiration from the whirling dance. May we continuously seek to deepen our connection with Allah and manifest His mercy and love in our actions. May the grace and wisdom of the whirling dance guide us towards inner peace, spiritual growth, and a greater understanding of our purpose in this world.

And Allah knows best.

Wa alaikum assalam warahmatullahi wabarakatuh (May the peace, mercy, and blessings of Allah be upon you).

*Sufi Secrets to Inner Healing………..*

## Section 9.2: Understanding Sama: The Whirling Meditation

Assalamu alaikum wa rahmatullahi wa barakatuhu (May the peace, mercy, and blessings of Allah be upon you),

My dear brothers and sisters,

In this section, we will be looking at the practice of Sama, also known as the Whirling Meditation. Sama holds a special place in Islamic spirituality, as it is a sacred and transformative journey towards attaining closeness to Allah and experiencing the depths of spiritual awakening. It is a practice that combines physical movement with spiritual devotion, and it has been embraced by Sufis as a means to reach higher states of consciousness.

Sama is not merely a physical dance or a spectacle to behold. It is a spiritual practice that is deeply rooted in the teachings of the Quran and the Hadith of our beloved Prophet Muhammad (peace be upon him). It is a way to engage the body, mind, and soul in a meditative and devotional state, enabling us to connect

*Sufi Secrets to Inner Healing...........*

with the Divine presence within ourselves and in the world around us.

In the Quran, Allah reminds us of the importance of remembering Him and seeking His remembrance through various means. Allah says in Surah Al-Jumu'ah (62:10), "And when the prayer is ended, then disperse in the land and seek of Allah's bounty, and remember Allah much, that you may be successful." Sama serves as a powerful form of remembrance, a vehicle through which we immerse ourselves in the Divine presence and seek closeness to Allah.

The practice of Sama finds its inspiration in the life and teachings of our Prophet Muhammad (peace be upon him). The Prophet Muhammad (peace be upon him) said, "Verily, in the remembrance of Allah do hearts find rest" (Recorded in Sahih Muslim). Sama allows us to engage in a form of remembrance that goes beyond words and enters the realm of experiential spirituality. Through the whirling movement, we can enter a state of deep meditation and connection with Allah.

*Sufi Secrets to Inner Healing...........*

The whirling movement itself is symbolic of the spiritual journey. Just as the dervishes spin, they are reminded of the ever-turning nature of life and the constant movement towards the Divine. It represents the soul's yearning for union with Allah and the journey towards spiritual perfection. The spinning motion also signifies the detachment from worldly attachments and the focus on the Divine presence.

In Sama, the dervishes often form a circle, representing unity and equality among participants. It is a powerful reminder that regardless of our backgrounds, social status, or worldly possessions, we are all equal in the eyes of Allah. It encourages us to let go of our egos, embrace humility, and foster a sense of unity and brotherhood.

Dear brothers and sisters, as an Islamic scholar and a seasoned preacher, I have personally witnessed the transformative power of Sama in the lives of individuals. It is not merely a physical act but a spiritual journey that can lead to profound healing, self-discovery, and a deeper understanding of our purpose in this

*Sufi Secrets to Inner Healing………..*

world. Through Sama, we can experience a sense of inner peace, spiritual elevation, and a closer connection with Allah.

However, it is important to note that Sama should be approached with the guidance of qualified teachers and within the framework of Islamic teachings. It is essential to maintain the proper intention, sincerity, and reverence towards Allah throughout the practice.

In conclusion, Sama, the Whirling Meditation, is a sacred practice that holds great spiritual significance in Islam. It is a means to remember Allah, seek His closeness, and embark on a transformative journey towards spiritual awakening. Through Sama, we can connect our physical movements with our spiritual devotion, allowing us to experience the depths of our faith and the beauty of our Islamic tradition.

*Sufi Secrets to Inner Healing...........*

## Section 9.3: Symbolism and Significance of the Whirling Dance

Bismillahir Rahmanir Raheem (In the name of Allah, the Most Gracious, the Most Merciful)

My dear brothers and sisters,

I will be discussing the symbolism and significance of the Whirling Dance, a practice that holds deep spiritual meaning in Islam. As an Islamic scholar and seasoned preacher, I have studied the Quran and the Hadith to uncover the wisdom and guidance that Allah has bestowed upon us regarding this profound form of expression and worship.

The Whirling Dance, often associated with the practice of Sufism, is a mesmerizing display of devotion and surrender. It involves the rhythmic spinning of the body, symbolizing the seeker's journey towards spiritual enlightenment and union with the Divine. In its captivating motions, the Whirling Dance carries powerful symbolism that can teach us valuable lessons about our relationship with Allah and our purpose in this world.

*Sufi Secrets to Inner Healing...........*

In Surah An-Nur (24:35), Allah says, "Allah is the Light of the heavens and the earth. The example of His light is like a niche within which is a lamp, the lamp is within glass, the glass as if it were a pearly [white] star lit from [the oil of] a blessed olive tree, neither of the east nor of the west, whose oil would almost glow even if untouched by fire. Light upon light. Allah guides to His light whom He wills. And Allah presents examples for the people, and Allah is Knowing of all things." This verse highlights the concept of Divine light and its reflection within us. The Whirling Dance can be seen as an expression of this inner light, as the seeker turns and spins, allowing the light of Allah to illuminate their being.

Additionally, the Whirling Dance represents the seeker's surrender to the Divine will. In Islam, we are taught to submit ourselves completely to Allah's guidance and trust in His plan for us. The spinning motion of the Whirling Dance symbolizes letting go of our ego, desires, and attachments to this world, and surrendering to the will of Allah. It reminds us that true freedom

*Sufi Secrets to Inner Healing…………*

and peace can only be attained through complete submission to our Creator.

In Surah Al-Anbiya (21:92), we are reminded of the Prophet Ibrahim's (peace be upon him) unwavering trust in Allah's guidance. Allah says, "And [Ibrahim] said, 'Indeed, I have turned my face toward He who created the heavens and the earth, inclining toward truth, and I am not of those who associate others with Allah.'" Ibrahim's example of complete devotion and surrender serves as an inspiration for us in our spiritual journey. The Whirling Dance, with its circular movements, echoes Ibrahim's turning towards the Divine and his unwavering faith.

Dear brothers and sisters, the Whirling Dance is not merely a physical spectacle; it is a profound spiritual practice that allows us to connect with Allah on a deeper level. As an Islamic scholar, I have witnessed the transformative power of the Whirling Dance in the lives of individuals. It has the potential to

*Sufi Secrets to Inner Healing...........*

awaken the heart, purify the soul, and facilitate a direct experience of the Divine presence.

It is important to note that the Whirling Dance should be practiced with the proper intention, guided by qualified teachers, and within the boundaries of Islamic teachings. The goal is to align our physical movements with our spiritual devotion, recognizing that the essence of the Whirling Dance lies in seeking closeness to Allah and purifying our hearts.

In conclusion, the Whirling Dance holds deep symbolism and significance in Islam. Through its graceful movements, it symbolizes our spiritual journey towards enlightenment, our surrender to Allah's will, and our striving for unity with the Divine. Let us embrace this sacred practice with reverence, understanding its profound teachings, and allowing us to experience a deeper connection with Allah.

The Whirling Dance reminds us of the profound truth that we are created to worship and seek closeness to Allah. It is a reminder that our existence is not limited to the physical realm,

*Sufi Secrets to Inner Healing………..*

but encompasses the spiritual dimensions as well. Through the Whirling Dance, we engage our bodies, minds, and souls in a harmonious union, aligning ourselves with the divine rhythm of the universe.

Furthermore, the Whirling Dance teaches us the importance of balance and harmony in our lives. Just as the dancer spins gracefully, maintaining equilibrium amidst the movement, we are reminded of the need to find balance in our spiritual and worldly pursuits. It urges us to seek moderation, avoiding extremes and excesses, and to live a life that is pleasing to Allah.

The Whirling Dance also carries the message of unity and interconnectedness. As the dancers spin in harmony, forming a circle, they demonstrate the oneness of humanity and our shared spiritual journey. It reminds us that despite our diverse backgrounds, cultures, and languages, we are all part of the ummah, the community of believers, united by our faith and devotion to Allah.

*Sufi Secrets to Inner Healing………..*

In Surah Al-Hujurat (49:13), Allah says, "O mankind, indeed We have created you from male and female and made you peoples and tribes that you may know one another. Indeed, the most noble of you in the sight of Allah is the most righteous of you. Indeed, Allah is Knowing and Acquainted." This verse emphasizes the importance of embracing diversity and building bridges of understanding among people. The Whirling Dance, with its inclusive nature, reminds us of our shared humanity and the importance of fostering unity and compassion in our interactions with others.

As an Islamic scholar and seasoned preacher, I have seen how the Whirling Dance can deeply touch the hearts of those who engage in it with sincerity and devotion. It has the power to awaken the dormant spiritual faculties within us, to heal our inner wounds, and to ignite a profound love for Allah and His creation.

However, it is essential to approach the Whirling Dance with reverence and understanding. Seek guidance from

*Sufi Secrets to Inner Healing………..*

knowledgeable teachers who can help you navigate its spiritual dimensions and ensure that it remains within the boundaries of Islamic teachings. Remember that the Whirling Dance is a means, not an end in itself, and its ultimate purpose is to draw us closer to Allah.

In conclusion, the Whirling Dance is a sacred practice that holds deep symbolism and significance in Islam. It is a powerful expression of our spiritual journey, surrender to Allah's will, and unity with the Divine and fellow believers. May we embrace this beautiful form of worship with humility, seeking Allah's pleasure and striving to deepen our connection with Him. May the Whirling Dance inspire us to embody the qualities of balance, harmony, unity, and love as we navigate our spiritual path in this world.

And Allah knows best.

Wa allahu ta'ala a'lam (And Allah knows best).

*Sufi Secrets to Inner Healing...........*

## Section 9.4: Experiencing Wholeness and Unity through Sama

Assalamu Alaikum wa rahmatullahi wa barakatuhu.

Dear brothers and sisters,

Follow me as I share with you the profound experience of experiencing wholeness and unity through Sama, the sacred practice of spiritual listening and music in Islam. As an Islamic scholar and seasoned preacher, I have witnessed the transformative power of Sama in the lives of believers and its ability to deepen their connection with Allah.

Sama is not merely a form of entertainment or a cultural tradition. It is a spiritual practice that aims to awaken our hearts, purify our souls, and bring us closer to our Creator. It is a beautiful expression of devotion and a means to experience the divine presence in our lives. When we engage in Sama with sincerity and humility, it can become a gateway to experiencing a sense of wholeness and unity.

*Sufi Secrets to Inner Healing...........*

In Surah Ar-Rum (30:21), Allah says, "And of His signs is that He created for you from yourselves mates that you may find tranquility in them; and He placed between you affection and mercy. Indeed in that are signs for a people who give thought." This verse reminds us of the importance of unity and love in our relationships. Sama, through its spiritual melodies and harmonies, allows us to connect with Allah's love and mercy, and in turn, foster love and compassion within ourselves and towards others.

The teachings of our beloved Prophet Muhammad (peace be upon him) also emphasize the significance of unity and brotherhood. In a well-known hadith, the Prophet (pbuh) said, "The believers are like a single body; if one part of it is afflicted with pain, the rest of the body will feel the discomfort." This hadith highlights the interconnectedness and unity of the believers. When we engage in Sama together, we experience a sense of oneness, transcending our individual identities and embracing the unity of the ummah.

*Sufi Secrets to Inner Healing………..*

Sama also allows us to experience a profound sense of spiritual wholeness. In the depths of our souls, we often feel fragmented and disconnected from our true nature. The distractions and challenges of this world can lead us astray, causing inner turmoil and disunity. However, through the melodies and rhythms of Sama, we are reminded of our spiritual essence and the need to seek unity within ourselves. Sama helps us align our hearts, minds, and actions with the divine purpose, bringing about a sense of inner peace and harmony.

As an Islamic scholar, I have personally witnessed the transformative power of Sama in the lives of individuals. I have seen tears of joy streaming down their faces as they immerse themselves in the melodies and lyrics that resonate with their souls. Sama has the ability to heal deep wounds, dispel feelings of loneliness and isolation, and ignite a flame of love and devotion for Allah.

However, it is important to approach Sama with knowledge and understanding. We must ensure that it remains within the

*Sufi Secrets to Inner Healing…………*

boundaries of Islamic teachings and is free from any practices that contradict our faith. Seek guidance from knowledgeable scholars and engage in Sama gatherings that uphold the principles of Islam.

In conclusion, Sama is a spiritual practice that enables us to experience wholeness and unity. Through its melodies, rhythms, and the devotion it inspires, we can deepen our connection with Allah, cultivate love and compassion, and find inner peace. Let us embrace this sacred practice with sincerity and humility, seeking Allah's pleasure and striving to become vessels of His love and mercy.

May Allah bless us all with the opportunity to experience the beauty of Sama and grant us spiritual wholeness and unity in our lives. May our hearts be filled with love, compassion, and devotion as we journey towards Him.

And Allah knows best.

Wa allahu ta'ala

*Sufi Secrets to Inner Healing...........*

# Chapter Ten

## Section 10.1: Conclusion: Living a Life of Inner Healing and Spiritual Well-being

Bismillahir Rahmanir Rahim.

Dear brothers and sisters,

As I conclude this series on living a life of inner healing and spiritual well-being, I am filled with gratitude for the opportunity to share these reflections with you. Throughout our journey, we have explored various aspects of our faith, delving into the teachings of the Holy Quran and the Hadith, seeking guidance and inspiration for our personal growth and development.

I have witnessed the transformative power of Islam in the lives of individuals. I have seen how the principles and teachings of our religion, when embraced wholeheartedly, have the ability to heal our inner wounds, restore our spiritual well-being, and bring us closer to Allah. It is my hope that the knowledge shared

*Sufi Secrets to Inner Healing...........*

in this series has served as a guiding light for each and every one of you.

In Surah Al-Isra (17:82), Allah says, "And We send down of the Quran that which is healing and mercy for the believers." This verse reminds us that the Quran is not just a book of guidance, but also a source of healing and mercy. Its verses have the power to touch our hearts, soothe our souls, and bring about a profound transformation within us. Through reflection, contemplation, and application of its teachings, we can find solace, peace, and healing for our inner selves.

Furthermore, the Prophet Muhammad (peace be upon him) has left us with a wealth of wisdom and guidance through his words and actions. His Hadiths serve as a beacon of light, offering practical advice and teachings on how to live a life of inner healing and spiritual well-being. One such Hadith states, "Whoever pursues a path seeking knowledge, Allah will make easy for him the path to Paradise." This Hadith reminds us of the

*Sufi Secrets to Inner Healing…………*

importance of seeking knowledge, not just in an academic sense, but also in the pursuit of spiritual growth and self-improvement.

Throughout this series, we have explored various themes, such as self-exploration, self-awareness, surrendering to divine will, embracing acceptance, acts of service and kindness, and the spiritual practices of Sama and Arabic calligraphy. Each of these topics holds profound significance in our journey of inner healing and spiritual well-being.

I have shared with you the Quranic verses and Hadiths that highlight the importance of these practices and their transformative impact on our lives. These teachings provide us with the guidance and direction we need to navigate the challenges of this world while striving for spiritual growth and attaining closeness to Allah.

Dear brothers and sisters, living a life of inner healing and spiritual well-being requires consistent effort and dedication. It is not a one-time accomplishment but rather a lifelong journey. We must continually strive to improve ourselves, seek

*Sufi Secrets to Inner Healing…………*

knowledge, practice self-reflection, engage in acts of worship, and maintain a strong connection with Allah.

Let us remember that our ultimate purpose in this world is to worship Allah and seek His pleasure. As we navigate the complexities of life, let us hold on firmly to the rope of Allah, seeking His guidance and relying on His mercy and forgiveness. Let us cultivate a heart filled with love, compassion, and gratitude, and let our actions reflect the beauty of our faith.

In conclusion, dear brothers and sisters, I am humbled to have shared this journey of inner healing and spiritual well-being with you. I pray that the knowledge and reflections shared in this series have been beneficial to you and have ignited a desire within your hearts to strive for a deeper connection with Allah.

May Allah bless us all with the strength and determination to live a life of inner healing and spiritual well-being. May He shower His mercy upon us, forgive our shortcomings, and guide us to the path of righteousness. May our actions and intentions be aligned with the teachings of the Quran and the Sunnah of

*Sufi Secrets to Inner Healing………..*

our beloved Prophet Muhammad (peace be upon him). May Allah grant us the wisdom to navigate the challenges of life and the resilience to overcome difficulties with patience and trust in His divine plan.

As we conclude this series, let us remember that our journey towards inner healing and spiritual well-being is a lifelong endeavor. It requires continuous self-reflection, self-improvement, and a deep connection with Allah. Dear brothers and sisters, I urge you to reflect on the lessons shared throughout this series and strive to implement them in your daily lives. Take the time to engage in acts of worship, seek knowledge, practice gratitude, show kindness and compassion towards others, and cultivate a heart that is filled with love and mercy.

Remember that Allah is always there for you, ready to listen to your prayers and offer guidance. Turn to Him in times of difficulty, seek solace in His words, and trust in His divine wisdom. Know that your journey towards inner healing and

*Sufi Secrets to Inner Healing...........*

spiritual well-being is unique, and Allah's mercy encompasses all aspects of your life.

In the words of the Prophet Muhammad (peace be upon him), "Verily, in the remembrance of Allah, hearts find rest." Let us make a conscious effort to increase our remembrance of Allah, for it is through this remembrance that we find tranquility and serenity in our hearts.

Dear brothers and sisters, I want to express my gratitude to all of you for joining me on this spiritual journey. It has been an honor and a privilege to share these reflections with you. May Allah accept our efforts, bless us with His mercy and forgiveness, and grant us success in this life and the Hereafter.

I leave you with the reminder to continue seeking knowledge, nurturing your faith, and striving for inner healing and spiritual well-being. May Allah guide you and bless you abundantly in all your endeavors.

Wa allahu ta'ala alam.

*Sufi Secrets to Inner Healing………..*

## Section 10.2: In the name of Allah, the Most Gracious, the Most Merciful.

Assalamu Alaikum wa Rahmatullahi wa Barakatuhu.

Dear brothers and sisters,

Welcome to this enlightening section where I will reflect upon the importance of embracing Sufi teachings in our everyday lives. As an Islamic scholar, I have had the privilege of studying the teachings of the Quran and the Sunnah, and I have witnessed the profound impact that Sufi teachings can have on an individual's spiritual journey.

Sufism, also known as tasawwuf, is a branch of Islamic spirituality that focuses on purifying the heart and attaining closeness to Allah. It emphasizes the inward journey, the development of noble character traits, and the cultivation of a deep and intimate connection with the Divine.

One of the fundamental teachings of Sufism is the concept of tawheed, the belief in the Oneness of Allah. In Surah Al-Ikhlas (Chapter 112), Allah says:

*Sufi Secrets to Inner Healing...........*

"Say, 'He is Allah, [who is] One, Allah, the Eternal Refuge. He neither begets nor is born, Nor is there to Him any equivalent.'"

This verse reminds us of the absolute unity and uniqueness of Allah. It teaches us to recognize and acknowledge His supreme power and to rely on Him alone in all aspects of our lives. Embracing this teaching enables us to let go of worldly attachments and surrender ourselves entirely to the will of Allah.

Sufi teachings also emphasize the purification of the heart from negative traits such as greed, jealousy, and arrogance, and the cultivation of positive qualities such as humility, love, and compassion. Prophet Muhammad (peace be upon him) said, "Verily, Allah does not look at your outward appearance or wealth, but rather He looks at your hearts and deeds." (Sahih Muslim)

This Hadith highlights the significance of purifying our hearts and striving to develop noble character traits. Sufi practices such as self-reflection, dhikr (remembrance of Allah), and

*Sufi Secrets to Inner Healing...........*

contemplation aid in this purification process, enabling us to align our hearts with the teachings of Islam.

Furthermore, Sufism emphasizes the importance of spiritual awakening and experiencing the presence of Allah in our daily lives. It teaches us to seek a deeper understanding of the Quran and to reflect upon its meanings. Allah says in Surah Al-Hadid (Chapter 57), verse 17:

"Know that Allah gives life to the earth after its lifelessness. We have made clear to you the signs; perhaps you will understand."

This verse encourages us to ponder over the signs of Allah's creation and His divine wisdom. By doing so, we can develop a profound appreciation for His existence and His infinite mercy.

In my personal experience as an Islamic scholar and a preacher, I have witnessed the transformative power of embracing Sufi teachings. Through dhikr and spiritual practices, I have witnessed individuals experiencing a deep sense of peace, tranquility, and closeness to Allah. Their lives have been enriched with a heightened awareness of the divine presence,

*Sufi Secrets to Inner Healing*………..

and their hearts have been filled with love and compassion for all of Allah's creation.

Dear brothers and sisters, it is essential for us to embrace Sufi teachings in our everyday lives. We should strive to purify our hearts, cultivate noble character traits, and seek a deeper connection with Allah. This can be achieved through regular acts of worship, sincere supplication, self-reflection, and the study of Islamic literature, including the works of Sufi scholars.

Let us remember that Sufi teachings are firmly rooted in the Quran and the Sunnah of the Prophet Muhammad (peace be upon him). They serve as a pathway to deepen our understanding of Islam and to develop a more profound relationship with Allah and His creation.

Embracing Sufi teachings in our everyday lives also means embodying the principles of compassion, humility, and service to others. Sufis believe that true spiritual growth is reflected in our actions towards fellow human beings. Prophet Muhammad (peace be upon him) said, "The most beloved of people to Allah

*Sufi Secrets to Inner Healing...........*

are those who are most beneficial to people." (Al-Mu'jam al-Awsat)

This Hadith emphasizes the importance of selflessness and kindness in our interactions with others. Sufis strive to embody these qualities by engaging in acts of charity, serving the less fortunate, and spreading love and kindness in their communities.

Furthermore, Sufism teaches us to develop a sense of detachment from worldly possessions and to focus on the eternal and spiritual aspects of life. This does not mean abandoning our responsibilities or neglecting our worldly duties. Rather, it encourages us to view material possessions as a means to serve Allah and His creation, rather than as an end in themselves.

In Surah Al-Isra (Chapter 17), verse 80, Allah says:

"And say: 'My Lord! Cause me to enter a sound entrance and to exit a sound exit. And grant me from Yourself a supporting authority.'"

*Sufi Secrets to Inner Healing...........*

This verse reminds us to seek Allah's guidance and support in all our endeavors. By embracing Sufi teachings, we develop a mindset of reliance on Allah and a recognition that our true success lies in His pleasure.

Dear brothers and sisters, incorporating Sufi teachings into our lives is not limited to a select group of individuals. It is a path that is open to every believer who seeks to deepen their spirituality and draw closer to Allah. Whether we are scholars, professionals, or homemakers, we can all benefit from the wisdom and guidance offered by Sufism.

In conclusion, embracing Sufi teachings in our everyday lives is an opportunity for us to enhance our spiritual well-being and draw closer to Allah. It involves purifying our hearts, cultivating noble character traits, seeking a deeper understanding of the Quran, and embodying compassion, humility, and service. By incorporating these teachings, we can transform ourselves into beacons of light and sources of goodness in the world.

*Sufi Secrets to Inner Healing………..*

May Allah bless us all with the ability to embrace Sufi teachings and to live a life of inner healing, spiritual well-being, and divine connection. Ameen.

And Allah knows best.

Assalamu Alaikum wa Rahmatullahi wa Barakatuhu.

## Section 10.3: Emotional and Spiritual Balance

Assalamu Alaikum wa Rahmatullahi wa Barakatuhu,

Dear brothers and sisters in faith,

In this final section of the Sufi Secret, I would like to share with you the importance of cultivating emotional and spiritual balance in our lives as believers. I have witnessed the transformative power of this practice and its profound impact on our well-being.

Emotional and spiritual balance refers to the ability to manage our emotions and maintain a harmonious state of mind, regardless of the circumstances we face. It involves finding inner peace, tranquility, and contentment by aligning our hearts and souls with the teachings of Islam.

Allah, in His infinite wisdom, has provided us with guidance in the Quran and through the teachings of Prophet Muhammad (peace be upon him) on how to achieve this balance. Let us delve into the depths of these teachings and gain insights into cultivating emotional and spiritual equilibrium.

*Sufi Secrets to Inner Healing………..*

## Seeking Refuge in Allah's Remembrance:

Allah says in the Quran, in Surah Ar-Ra'd (Chapter 13), verse 28:

"Those who have believed and whose hearts are assured by the remembrance of Allah. Unquestionably, by the remembrance of Allah, hearts are assured."

When we engage in the remembrance of Allah, through acts of worship such as prayer, recitation of the Quran, and supplication, we find solace and tranquility in His presence. This connection with our Creator helps us navigate through the ups and downs of life with a calm and balanced mindset.

## Trusting in Allah's Decree:

In Surah Al-Baqarah (Chapter 2), verse 216, Allah says:

"But perhaps you hate a thing and it is good for you; and perhaps you love a thing and it is bad for you. And Allah knows, while you know not."

*Sufi Secrets to Inner Healing………..*

This verse reminds us of the importance of placing our trust in Allah's decree, even when we face challenges or difficulties. Cultivating emotional and spiritual balance requires us to have faith in Allah's wisdom and to accept His plan for us, knowing that He knows what is best for us.

**Practicing Gratitude:**

Expressing gratitude is a powerful tool in cultivating emotional and spiritual balance. Allah says in Surah An-Nisa (Chapter 4), verse 147:

"What can Allah gain by your punishment if you are grateful and believe? And ever is Allah Appreciative and Knowing."

By recognizing and acknowledging the blessings bestowed upon us by Allah, we develop a positive outlook on life and cultivate contentment in our hearts. Gratitude shifts our focus from what is lacking to what we have been blessed with, thereby nurturing emotional balance and inner peace.

*Sufi Secrets to Inner Healing………..*

## Controlling Anger:

Prophet Muhammad (peace be upon him) advised us to control our anger. He said, "The strong is not the one who overcomes the people by his strength, but the strong is the one who controls himself while in anger." (Sahih al-Bukhari)

By restraining our anger and responding with patience and forgiveness, we not only maintain emotional balance within ourselves but also foster harmonious relationships with others. Islam teaches us the importance of self-control and managing our emotions in a constructive manner.

## Seeking Knowledge:

Islam encourages the pursuit of knowledge as a means to attain spiritual growth and emotional well-being. Seeking knowledge allows us to gain a deeper understanding of our faith and provides us with tools to navigate life's challenges. Allah says in Surah Al-Mujadilah (Chapter 58), verse 11:

*Sufi Secrets to Inner Healing……….*

"Allah will raise those who have believed among you and those who were given knowledge by degrees. And Allah is Acquainted with what you do."

By continuously seeking knowledge, we equip ourselves with the necessary guidance to cultivate emotional and spiritual balance in our lives. We can engage in the study of the Quran, the teachings of the Prophet Muhammad (peace be upon him), and the works of Islamic scholars to deepen our understanding of Islam and its teachings on emotional and spiritual well-being.

**Self-Reflection and Self-Improvement:**

Self-reflection is an essential practice in cultivating emotional and spiritual balance. It involves introspection, assessing our actions and intentions, and seeking ways to improve ourselves. Allah says in Surah Al-Hujurat (Chapter 49), verse 13:

"O mankind, indeed We have created you from male and female and made you peoples and tribes that you may know one another. Indeed, the most noble of you in the sight of Allah is

*Sufi Secrets to Inner Healing………..*

the most righteous of you. Indeed, Allah is Knowing and Acquainted."

By examining our character, identifying areas for growth, and striving to become better individuals, we can enhance our emotional well-being and strengthen our connection with Allah.

**Practicing Forgiveness and Compassion:**

Forgiveness and compassion are integral to cultivating emotional and spiritual balance. Allah says in Surah Al-Imran (Chapter 3), verse 134:

"Those who spend [in the cause of Allah] during ease and hardship and who restrain anger and who pardon the people - and Allah loves the doers of good."

By forgiving others and showing compassion, we release ourselves from the burden of negativity and foster inner peace. It is through acts of kindness and mercy that we embody the teachings of Islam and contribute to a more harmonious and compassionate society.

*Sufi Secrets to Inner Healing...........*

In conclusion, dear brothers and sisters, cultivating emotional and spiritual balance is a lifelong journey. By incorporating these teachings from the Quran and the Sunnah into our daily lives, we can experience profound inner healing and spiritual well-being. Let us strive to seek refuge in Allah's remembrance, trust in His decree, practice gratitude, control our anger, seek knowledge, engage in self-reflection, and embody forgiveness and compassion.

May Allah guide us all on this path of balance and grant us emotional and spiritual well-being. May He fill our hearts with tranquility, contentment, and love for Him and for one another. Ameen.

And Allah knows best.

Wa Alaikum Assalam wa Rahmatullahi wa Barakatuhu.

*Sufi Secrets to Inner Healing………..*

## Section 10.4: The Eternal Journey of Inner Healing and Transformation

Bismillahir Rahmanir Rahim (In the name of Allah, the Most Gracious, the Most Merciful).

Dear brothers and sisters in Islam,

I am super elated as I end with this section on the eternal journey of inner healing and transformation. This journey is a profound and transformative experience that takes us closer to our Creator and enables us to attain spiritual growth and well-being. It is a journey that requires self-reflection, self-improvement, and a deep connection with the teachings of the Quran and the Sunnah of our beloved Prophet Muhammad (peace be upon him).

**Recognizing the Need for Inner Healing:**

In order to embark on this eternal journey of inner healing and transformation, we must first recognize the need for it. We live in a world filled with distractions, temptations, and hardships

*Sufi Secrets to Inner Healing...........*

that can leave us spiritually and emotionally wounded. Allah reminds us in Surah Al-Sharh (Chapter 94), verse 5-6:

"Indeed, with hardship, there is ease. Indeed, with hardship, there is ease."

These verses remind us that despite the challenges we face, Allah has provided us with the means to heal and find solace in Him. It is through our acknowledgment of our weaknesses and shortcomings that we can begin the process of inner healing.

**Seeking Allah's Guidance and Mercy:**

As we embark on this journey, we must seek Allah's guidance and mercy. Allah says in Surah Al-Isra (Chapter 17), verse 82:

"And We send down of the Quran that which is healing and mercy for the believers."

The Quran is a source of healing and guidance for us. It contains verses that address our emotional and spiritual well-being. It is through the recitation and contemplation of the Quran that we can find solace, guidance, and healing for our hearts and souls.

*Sufi Secrets to Inner Healing………..*

Developing a Personal Relationship with Allah:

In order to experience inner healing and transformation, it is crucial to develop a personal relationship with Allah. This relationship is nurtured through acts of worship, such as prayer, fasting, and supplication. Allah says in Surah Al-Baqarah (Chapter 2), verse 186:

"And when My servants ask you concerning Me, indeed I am near. I respond to the invocation of the supplicant when he calls upon Me."

By turning to Allah in sincere supplication and seeking His guidance, we open the doors of mercy and healing in our lives. It is through this connection with our Creator that we find strength, peace, and comfort during times of distress.

**Embracing Patience and Trust:**

Throughout our journey of inner healing and transformation, we will encounter challenges and tests. It is during these moments

*Sufi Secrets to Inner Healing...........*

that we must embrace patience and trust in Allah's wisdom and plan. Allah says in Surah Al-Baqarah (Chapter 2), verse 153:

"O you who have believed, seek help through patience and prayer. Indeed, Allah is with the patient."

By demonstrating patience and turning to Allah in prayer, we can find solace and strength to overcome difficulties. It is through our trust in Allah's divine decree that we can experience true inner healing and transformation.

**Purifying the Heart:**

As we travel on this eternal journey, it is essential to purify our hearts from negative traits and emotions. The Prophet Muhammad (peace be upon him) said in a hadith:

"Indeed, in the body, there is a piece of flesh, which if it is sound, the entire body will be sound, and if it is corrupt, the entire body will be corrupt. Indeed, it is the heart."

The heart is the center of our emotions and spiritual well-being. By purifying our hearts from envy, anger, pride, and other

*Sufi Secrets to Inner Healing………..*

negative traits, we can attain inner peace and spiritual balance. The Quran provides guidance on purifying the heart and attaining inner peace. Allah says in Surah Al-Hujurat (Chapter 49), verse 13:

"O mankind, indeed We have created you from male and female and made you peoples and tribes that you may know one another. Indeed, the most noble of you in the sight of Allah is the most righteous of you. Indeed, Allah is Knowing and Acquainted."

This verse emphasizes the importance of righteousness and character in the sight of Allah. By cultivating positive qualities such as compassion, forgiveness, and humility, we purify our hearts and draw closer to Allah.

**Practicing Self-Reflection and Self-Improvement:**

On this eternal journey, self-reflection plays a vital role. It is through introspection and self-awareness that we can identify our flaws and areas in need of improvement. The Prophet Muhammad (peace be upon him) said in a hadith:

*Sufi Secrets to Inner Healing………..*

"Take account of yourselves before you are taken to account, weigh your deeds before they are weighed for you."

By taking a moment to assess our actions, thoughts, and intentions, we can strive for self-improvement and seek forgiveness for our shortcomings. This process of self-reflection allows us to grow spiritually and attain inner healing.

**Seeking Knowledge and Wisdom:**

Knowledge is a key component of our journey towards inner healing and transformation. The Quran encourages us to seek knowledge and gain wisdom. Allah says in Surah Al-Zumar (Chapter 39), verse 9:

"Say, 'Are those who know equal to those who do not know?' Only they will remember [who are] people of understanding."

By acquiring knowledge of the Quran, Hadith, and Islamic teachings, we equip ourselves with the tools necessary for self-improvement and spiritual growth. It is through this knowledge

*Sufi Secrets to Inner Healing..........*

that we gain a deeper understanding of Allah's guidance and His plan for us.

**Spreading Love and Kindness:**

As we continue on this eternal journey, it is essential to spread love and kindness to others. The Prophet Muhammad (peace be upon him) said in a hadith:

"None of you truly believes until he loves for his brother what he loves for himself."

By showing compassion, empathy, and generosity towards others, we contribute to the well-being of our communities and promote harmony and unity. Through acts of kindness, we can inspire others to embark on their own journey of inner healing and transformation.

In conclusion, dear brothers and sisters, the eternal journey of inner healing and transformation is a lifelong endeavor. It requires sincere effort, self-reflection, and a deep connection with Allah. By seeking His guidance, purifying our hearts, and

*Sufi Secrets to Inner Healing………..*

practicing love and kindness, we can experience the beauty and depth of spiritual growth and attain inner peace and well-being.

May Allah bless us all on this journey and grant us the strength and perseverance to continue seeking His pleasure. Ameen.

Assalamu Alaikum wa rahmatullahi wa barakatuh.

*Sufi Secrets to Inner Healing………..*

# Appreciation

Dear valued readers,

Assalamu Alaikum wa rahmatullahi wa barakatuh.

I would like to take a moment to express my heartfelt appreciation to each and every one of you. Your dedication to seeking knowledge, your commitment to personal growth, and your presence here today are a testament to your unwavering love for Islam and your desire to deepen your understanding of emotional and spiritual well-being.

Throughout this book, I have endeavored to present the teachings of Sufism in a comprehensive and accessible manner, drawing upon the wisdom of the Holy Quran and the Hadiths. It is my sincere hope that the words written within these pages have resonated with you, providing guidance, inspiration, and a renewed sense of faith.

Your engagement and enthusiasm have been a source of great encouragement for me as an Islamic scholar and seasoned preacher. Your willingness to explore the depths of Sufi

*Sufi Secrets to Inner Healing………..*

teachings and your openness to embracing emotional and spiritual healing have demonstrated your commitment to personal transformation.

I am humbled by the opportunity to share my knowledge and personal experiences with you. It is my belief that as we journey together through the chapters of this book, we are not just gaining knowledge but also forging a deeper connection with our Creator and discovering the immense potential for inner healing and spiritual growth that lies within each of us.

Please know that your dedication to seeking emotional and spiritual well-being is a testament to your faith and your desire to live a life in accordance with the teachings of Islam. By prioritizing the nurturing of your soul, you are contributing to the betterment of yourself, your families, and your communities.

May Allah, the Most Merciful, shower you with His abundant blessings and guide you on the path of emotional and spiritual well-being. May He grant you the strength to overcome

*Sufi Secrets to Inner Healing...........*

challenges, the wisdom to navigate life's complexities, and the inner peace that comes from surrendering to His will.

Once again, I extend my heartfelt appreciation to each and every one of you for embarking on this journey with me. Your commitment to personal growth and your dedication to living a life of emotional and spiritual well-being is truly inspiring. May Allah bless you abundantly and may the knowledge gained from this book continue to illuminate your path.

With gratitude and warm regards,

**Hanifa Ibn Al-Nawawi**

"السلامة مع"

(ma'a as-salamah).

Printed in Poland
by Amazon Fulfillment
Poland Sp. z o.o., Wrocław